In *The Uncomfortable C*   )ctor
of the Church." That   ⎿ the
sense that "doctor" me   :om-
passion, wisdom, and authority, as I've read carefully every word of his
manuscript. For every one of us as members of a hurting, broken human
family, this is a "must" read. It is well worth the concentrated effort necessary to follow the Doctor's irrefutable logic. My prayer is that God's
Doctor, the Holy Spirit, will illuminate truth to each mind and heart.

REV. DAVID MAINSE, FOUNDER, 100 HUNTLEY STREET AND CROSSROADS
TELEVISION SYSTEM; DISTINGUISHED INTERNATIONAL CHRISTIAN BROADCASTER

For over twenty years, my denomination (The United Church of
Canada) has endured controversy and hard feelings over issues of homosexual behaviour and its relationship to the mind and will of God. Offi-
cially, it has concluded that homosexuality is a "gift of God."
Subsequently, orthodox and evangelical Christians who hold to a more
traditional and biblical view of sexuality have often been labelled as
homophobic and even persecuted. This story has been a very painful
one to live through for many. Larry Brice offers a comprehensive survey
and careful reading of scripture, which reminds us not only of the Bible's
clear teaching on sexual behaviour, but also of Christ's call to love one
another as he has loved us.

REV. WILLIAM HOUGHTON, BA, MDIV, THM
THE UNITED CHURCH OF CANADA, COLLIER ST.
UNITED CHURCH, BARRIE, ONTARIO

Larry Brice pulls no punches in his plea to traditionalists and evangelicals
to be reconciled with and to welcome homosexuals into their midst.
Larry does not in any way reduce the significance of what the Bible tells
us of the sanctity of marriage and the dangers of practicing sexual freedom, while he offers his love to Christians who have faced alienation and
rejection due to their sexual orientation. But he calls for more than the
acceptance of the person. He also outlines a practical down-to-earth way
to work through sexual temptations in order for each child of God to

fully express their God-given talents. Sexual orientation is a difficult and volatile subject, ripping apart many denominations and nullifying the voice of the church in the public arena. Larry provides spiritual and practical insights that would serve the church well in dealing with this derisive topic.

Dr. R. Gary Chiang, BSc, MSc, PhD

AUTHOR; INTERNATIONALLY RECOGNIZED PROFESSOR OF BIOLOGY,

REDEEMER UNIVERSITY COLLEGE, ANCASTER, ON, CANADA

As Larry identifies and wrestles with issues dividing Christians in North America for the last fifty years in regard to homosexuality, he pleads for the evangelical, conservative branch of the Christian church to maintain a traditional Biblical interpretation on heterosexual and homosexual activity, while also challenging Christians to repent of the hatred and bigotry with which they have treated homosexual persons. He yearns for terms of peace to be established so that the church as a whole will not continue to be torn apart but might regain its prophetic voice. I appreciate Larry's heart for the gospel, the church, and for all people regardless of sexual orientation.

John Howard, BA, MDiv, OACCPP, AACC

INDIVIDUAL, MARRIAGE, AND FAMILY THERAPIST; RECOVERED HOMOSEXUAL

Not many pastors are willing to talk about homosexuality, let alone write a book about it. Dr. Brice wades into a very 'uncomfortable' topic for the church, but he handles it well by striking a skillful balance between conviction and compassion. I appreciate how he tows the line of Scripture but also tugs at the heart of his readers with his passionate challenge—to not just stay true to God's Word on marriage, but also to God's mission of reconciliation. This book is an honest plea to the church to deal with the discomfort of homosexuality faithfully but lovingly, and it's a message the church needs to hear.

Kent DelHousaye, BA, MDiv, DMin CANDIDATE

TEACHING PASTOR, BETHANY BIBLE CHURCH; ADJUNCT PROFESSOR,

GRAND CANYON UNIVERSITY, ARIZONA

The Uncomfortable Church

DR. LAWRENCE BRICE

THE
UNCOMFORTABLE
CHURCH

Can Gays Be Reconciled to the Body of Christ?

Deep River
B O O K S

The Uncomfortable Church
Can Gays Be Reconciled to the Body of Christ
Copyright © 2013 by Dr. Lawrence Brice

All rights reserved. No part of this book may be reproduced or transmitted in any form or by any means, electronic or mechanical, including photocopying and recording, or by any information storage and retrieval system, without permission in writing from the publisher.

Unless otherwise marked, all Scripture quotations are taken from the *New Revised Standard Version Bible,* copyright ©1989, Division of Christian Education of the National Council of the Churches of Christ in the United States of America. Used by permission. All rights reserved.

Scripture quotations marked "KJV" are taken from The King James Version of the Bible.

Scripture quotations marked NIV are taken from the *Holy Bible, New International Version*® NIV®. Copyright © 1973, 1978, 1984 by International Bible Society. Used by permission of Zondervan. All rights reserved.

Scripture quotations marked NASB are taken from the *New American Standard Bible,* © Copyright 1960, 1962, 1963, 1968, 1971, 1972, 1973, 1975, 1977, 1995 by The Lockman Foundation. Used by permission.

Scripture quotations marked "ESV" are taken from *The Holy Bible, English Standard Version.* Copyright © 2000; 2001 by Crossway Bibles, a division of Good News Publishers. Used by permission. All rights reserved.

DEEP RIVER BOOKS
Sisters, Oregon
www.deepriverbooks.com

ISBN-13: 9781937756697
ISBN-10: 1937756696

Library of Congress: 2012952903

Cover design by David Litwin, Purefusion Media

❧

This book is dedicated to the extraordinary love in my life, my wife Karen, with the prayer that all those reading it will find joy in their relationships as I have continuously found in God's eminent gift of Christian marriage. Together, we make one strong person.

ACKNOWLEDGMENTS

For years my wife Karen has shared her thoughts, prayers, and insightful conversation with me on many topics concerning gays and lesbians. Karen is not just my partner in marriage but a colleague in the study of homosexuality, for which I am deeply enriched and grateful.

Once the book was finished and I gave it into the hands of the Lord, I heard of the Deep River Books competition for the best manuscripts for publication. I entered and was delighted when I heard that I had been a finalist, winning the Award of Merit.

Deep River Books gives new authors a place in the publishing industry, and I am grateful for it. I want to thank the publishers of Deep River Books, Bill and Nancie Carmichael, for their enthusiastic encouragement and for the burning vision we share for ministries of reconciliation.

What a team at Deep River Books for achieving excellence, with everything from design, marketing, public relations, publicity, cover, and editing. Kit Tosello and Rhonda Funk, your contributions are immeasurable to us authors! We love you back!

When I won the Award of Merit from Deep River Books for this manuscript, I had a feeling that this might be a good book. However, after Rachel Starr Thomson did all her hard work to edit meticulously down to the finest details in the manuscript, I began to feel that *The Uncomfortable Church* might even become a great book! Thanks, Rachel, for giving style, structure, and hope to your authors.

My sincere thanks to Sandy Young, Bill Wiebe, John Howard, and Will Haughton for your encouragement in being the first to read the manuscript, and for your unfailing friendships!

Special thanks to those who gave of their time to write with passion their endorsements for this book. Also, my literary agent, Kimberly Shumate, fired the starting pistol when I first suggested writing a book on reconciling gays to the church. Thanks, Kimberly!

Finally, I want to witness to and worship the faithful God and Savior who called this Jonah to his Nineveh of homosexuality, as I also continue my prayers for all those in same-sex relationships: that you too will discover the love, grace, and peace of the Lord Jesus Christ! It is my prayer that you will be able to say with all of us in the body of Christ, *"Agnus Dei, qui tollis peccatu mundi, miserere nobis"* (see John 1:29). Hopefully all the readers of this book will be able to say with me a silent amen.

TABLE OF CONTENTS

Introduction 13

Chapter 1: Ending the Battle 17
God calls a pastor to speak to the churches about
sexual relationships.

Chapter 2: Overview of Sexuality in the Bible 27
The Bible affirms that God made us all the way
we are. Is there a divine trajectory for sexual relations?

Chapter 3: Homosexuality in the Old Testament:
Battling a Giant 51
Is homosexuality indelibly written in the Old Testament as a sin
so that it cannot be completely erased as such? Two Reformed
giants battle it out.

Chapter 4: Homosexuality in the New Testament 71
How and where does the New Testament refer to gays? Is there a
credible and entirely persuasive reply to the revisionist, liberal
interpretation of Scripture?

Chapter 5: Gays, Lesbians, and St. Paul 81
Does the apostle Paul describe homosexuality in Romans 1:18–32
in a way consistent with what we find in same-sex relationships
today, or does Paul only conform to Old Testament Scriptures?

Chapter 6: The Definition of Marriage and the Role of
Civil Rights 97
What overarching and predominant nature does opposite-gender
marriage have compared to same-sex relationships, and do the
issues of equality and civil rights trump everything else in the marriage debate?

Chapter 7: Pastoral Care of Gays and Lesbians 113

Evangelicals have often fallen off the "game plan" given in the gospel in battling with the homosexual community. This chapter addresses the positive side of care and outreach to gays and lesbians that builds bridges for reconciliation with the body of Christ.

Chapter 8: Here Is the Mission Field 129

The church has a clear choice: accept the gay community without change into the church, or accept gays and lesbians while always holding on to their potential to become what Jesus and the Bible say they can become. We hear the testimony of two ex-gays as ideal examples of what this encounter between gays and the evangelical church looks like.

Chapter 9: The Terms of Peace: The Future of Gays in
the Church 143

Here's what evangelicals can offer to the gay, lesbian, bisexual, and transgender community and their ecclesiastical supporters, and what the orthodox believing church must maintain. The body of Christ faces the extreme risk of Christians attacking Christians so badly over homosexuality that it could result in something like the history of the fall of Constantinople to the barbarians—and the consequential destruction of any Christian's ability to speak prophetically to the nation about God's plan for love, sex, and marriage—even imperiling the credibility of the gospel itself.

Endnotes 157

INTRODUCTION

The title *The Uncomfortable Church* testifies to the intense ecclesiastical battle over gay and lesbian ordination and marriage and how awkward many Christians feel in this debate. Some in the mainline Christian denominations are battle weary and willing to agree to almost anything just to make the problem go away. However, the issue of the morality of same-gender sexual relations is still the elephant in the room for many Christians today. It seems that most Protestant denominations can deal comfortably with, and even be reconciled to, those who commit adultery or even murder, or who struggle with addictions, but when gays and lesbians come into the church, it is different. They often wear their homosexuality on their sleeve and cannot, or do not want to, hide their identity when they come out in public. Coming into many local congregations, gays truly sense they have come into "the uncomfortable church."

Can gays be reconciled to the body of Christ? This book differs from the liberal, revisionist apologetic that demands theological change to the point of schism. I believe that conservative, evangelical Christians can end the war with many in the gay community without abandoning the clearest and most compelling interpretation of Scripture or leaving the biblical culture of evangelicals, whose everyday lives reflect the beliefs and values of the Bible. This book attempts to open up a new front in these ecclesiastical discussions, helping us to reach new comfort levels in the church with the truest and most authentic terms of peace.

This book is written for Christians who want to know and believe the clearest and most comprehensive interpretation of the Bible's moral teaching in regard to sexual relationships outside the marriage of a man and a woman. In these pages, I have endeavored to give sensitive answers to this question for Christian leaders and laity, to help them know with convincing conviction, from Scripture and reason, the answers to the morality of homosexuality.

For some decades now, the Christian church has been awash in controversy over this issue, as some mainline denominations have given their approval to homosexual ordination and marriage even as others dig their heels in and roundly condemn both the lifestyle and the individuals who practice it. I pray this book will inform many Christians in churches, including ministers—and not just young ministers—who have forgotten or lost sight of the reasons why the church once rejected gay marriage and ordination.

It is possible that the whole controversy around these issues will tone down and become more commonplace with the passing of the years, falling out in different levels of acceptance and resistance by the Protestant denominations. Yet whatever position the churches in North America ultimately take, it is my fervent hope that this book, from the heart of the body of Christ by a doctor of the church, will help evangelical and mainline Christians to firmly answer the moral questions on love, sex, and marriage. With a firm moral answer beneath our feet, all of us will be free to adjust to and welcome gays and lesbians in whatever way we think appropriate.

Hopefully we can all move beyond our discomfort into faithful love, true Christian unity, and effective pastoral care that will demonstrate the many important ways in which gays and lesbians can be reconciled to the body of Christ.

We begin with the most important resource, the authority of Scripture, considering the many and varied attempts to reinterpret—or even to set aside—the Bible on homosexuality. Although Scripture's clear teaching is often seen as irrelevant to the committed, loving, and faithful same-gender couples in some churches today, we must answer the question of whether, in God's Word, marriage between a man and a woman is the only acceptable venue for sexual activity. A careful reading of Scripture's plain meaning may be mocked and scorned as antigay, but shouldn't it represent the foremost concern for those to whom the Bible is the official guide for faith and life?[1]

The Scriptures are so important to all branches of the Christian churches that even the liberals and the revisionists know they must support any changes to church doctrine with a persuasive interpretation of the Holy Bible. It is in the Scriptures that we will find our best answers to our questions on sexual relations. We start this book in chapters 2, 3, 4, and 5 with the essential search for answers from Scripture.

For those in conservative churches who are "uncomfortable" with same-sex couples and are at a loss to understand how to accept and love those whose lifestyles are so antithetical to their worldview, chapters 7 and 8 will introduce ex-gays and lesbians through whom evangelicals can comfortably come face-to-face with the homosexual world and realize that there is a clear way to love them, preparing the church to encounter and minister to its mission field of homosexuals who don't know the Lord.

For Christians dealing with legislators, those facing gay rights in the courts, and those wishing to communicate their beliefs in the public sphere where Scripture does not hold the authority it does in the church, chapter 6, on "natural law" and the nature of traditional marriage, will shed light on the important question of whether the traditional and historic definition of marriage as the union of one man and one woman can be trumped by the popular imperative of gay "equality" and civil rights.

To those likely to disagree with me, I humbly ask for an open mind and for a careful reading of the whole book, with special attention to its conclusions and "the terms of peace" in chapter 9. Everyone needs to know what we conservatives firmly believe and the consequences for changing the doctrine on sex, marriage, and homosexuality.

This book thrusts the different traditions and institutions of Protestant Christianity toward reconciliation with the gay, lesbian, bisexual, and transgender (GLBT) community. It makes a bold attempt to lead Christ-centered conservatives to understand what we cannot and will not change, and why we won't, and yet still grant concessions that revisionists are looking for—without creating a revolution or a schism within the churches. It is my sincere desire that this book will help the body of Christ find ways to reconcile on many positive issues with gays and lesbians, with the different sides dialoguing together and discussing the very best that each has to contribute to the work of God's kingdom on earth.

Chapter 1

ENDING THE BATTLE

I have been a practicing minister and a doctor of the church for over thirty years in the historic Christian denomination known as the Presbyterian Church in Canada. I am also an evangelist. I have had an international preaching ministry for over twenty years, and more recently, have been broadcasting nationally on network television across Canada and internationally on affiliate stations in the US and overseas, interviewing Christian leaders from Canada and internationally since 2003.

For the two decades of the 1990s and the 2000s, I sat silently, not wanting to speak out, observing the drama of the unfolding debate and controversy over the place of gays and lesbians in the church. That debate is recorded as much in the annals of major Christian denominations as it is in the daily newspapers.

It must be said here that I am one who has changed his mind. I tried to lead my denomination at its General Assembly in 1985 to adopt a positive position toward gay rights, hoping it would lead to gay ordination and marriage. I will describe this a little later, but for now will say that when my bride and I began to intensely read, study, and pray over the Bible together every weekday morning during the first five years of our marriage before children, these creative, inspiring years changed my views until I no longer approved of gay sexual relations.

Awareness in North America for the gay movement began early in the 1960s. As Wikipedia records:

> Gay liberation is the name used to describe the lesbian, gay, bisexual and transgender movement of the late 1960s and early to mid 1970s in North America, Western Europe, and Australia and New Zealand.

Gay lib is also known for its links to the counterculture of the time, and for the Gay liberationists' intent to transform fundamental institutions of society such as gender and the family. In order to achieve such liberation, consciousness raising and direct action were employed. By the late 1970s, the radicalism of Gay liberation was eclipsed by a return to a more formal movement that espoused gay and lesbian civil rights.[2]

By the 1970s, the gay rights movement began to receive attention from some Christian denominations, such as the United Church of Canada. In 2003, that denomination, to the dismay of its orthodox and evangelical ministers, approved homosexuality as "a gift from God." Now the pro-gay lobby has its equivalent in the pro-gay Christian movement, as other major Protestant denominations, like the Anglican Church of Canada and the Episcopal Church in the USA, have legitimized gay, lesbian, bisexual, and transgender sexual activity as morally equal to that between heterosexual married people. A more detailed history of the gay rights movement will be given in chapter 7.

A Building Storm

After much thought and the reading of Scripture that led me to change my mind, and perceiving where this debate might be going as gay men came into my congregation and I annually witnessed the largest gay pride parades in the world in my home city of Toronto, I wrestled with how to find common ground with the gay, lesbian, bisexual, and transgender community. But I sat completely powerless on the sidelines, watching this sexual and theological crisis unfold.

Sometimes God captures a pastor and brings him to a complete stop as he reads Scripture. A passage can jump right off the page with the same power with which the Holy Spirit impacted the author who wrote it in the first place. That happened to me in the area of homosexuality and the church, and hence the writing of this book. Let me explain.

Television opinion polls and published national statistics for several decades have evidenced a building crisis for many clergy over the decline of the "traditional family," as we've seen married couples with children decrease and become the minority in the family structures in North America. For most of us, alarm bells began to ring louder as we started to hear more and more the popular refrain that there is no need for heterosexual couples to wait until after marriage to share sexual intimacy and cohabit, so that now any sexual relationship between consenting adults is approved of. And many denominations had nothing to say to the nation in this debacle—except the attempt from some churches to be more inclusive and accepting of social change.

With most churches having widely missed this huge target of heterosexual immorality, many clergy and lay leaders in mainline Christian denominations now want to run away from the uncomfortable homosexual debate and are looking for an easy place to land, even if the only room on this precarious ledge is with the liberal revisionists and their reinterpretation of Scripture.

For some of us clergy, the sense of crisis and outrage continued to amplify with what seemed like the ecclesiastical abandonment of this moral disaster. It seemed like the mainline churches lost their courage to lead their churches and the nation in promoting godly single lives of virginity and celibacy and instead taught them to succumb to the media mantra of "responsible sex" as the only morality outside marriage. What could a pastor, or his or her denomination, do? An overwhelming sense of helplessness and weak resignation deepened in my heart.

As I always do under these kinds of circumstances, I asked God for a Scripture to comfort me and help me find my way. God immediately responded, and he struck with such impact that it led to the writing of this book. My Bible opened to Proverbs 24:10–12:

> If you faint in the day of adversity,
> your strength being small;
> if you hold back from rescuing those taken away to death,
> those who go staggering to the slaughter;
> if you say, "Look, we did not know this"—
> does not he who weighs the heart perceive it?

Does not he who keeps watch over your soul know it?
And will he not repay all according to their deeds?

I remembered that these were the same verses missionary Hudson Taylor read as his ship left dock to journey across the ocean for China, where he would begin his astonishing work of evangelism. God convicted him through this passage not to be weak or fainthearted in his overwhelming call. Hudson Taylor, possibly feeling crushed by the immensity of his task, had to answer God's words to not faint or fail in his almost inconceivable task on "the day of adversity."

I knew from the book of Proverbs that this passage also refers back to an earlier passage, where a father warns his son to save him from sexual immorality:

My child, if you accept my words…
You will be saved from the loose woman, from the adulteress with her smooth words…for her way leads down *to death,*
and her path *to the shades;*
those who go to her *never come back,*
nor do they regain the paths of life.

PROVERBS 2:1, 16–19, EMPHASIS MINE. SEE ALSO PROVERBS 5:1–23

In the Bible, sexual immorality most frequently refers to heterosexual promiscuity and adultery, as in the above passage, but the Bible does speak to the whole range of sexually questionable morality, including homosexuality.

So many times, I struggled against writing this book—until I read these verses in Proverbs. I knew the intensity and stress of those participating in the gay rights controversy, and like Jonah wanting to escape God's call to preach to desperate Nineveh, I wanted to run away from God's calling to take any active role in this sensitive and explosive issue. But God compelled me, from these verses in Proverbs, to dig in, research, and hold to a strong biblical position.

ENDING THE BATTLE

A CHANGE OF MIND

In the early 1980s, I approved of homosexual acts as morally acceptable and natural. I believed them to be morally right because I bought into the idea that homosexuality was as normal as having red hair and as unchangeable as the color of your skin. If God made people this way, with God-given sexual urges, then it was a natural and moral thing for everyone to accept it. Already in the 1980s these ideas were beginning to appear in popular newspaper columns, even in trusted family favorites such as Ann Landers.

The year after I was married, in 1985, I was a commissioner at the General Assembly of the Presbyterian Church in Canada in Guelph, Ontario, when our Church Doctrine Committee made its first report on homosexuality. After the report made to our national court recommended against the ecclesiastical approval of same-gender sexual relationships, ending with the words that this report should become the policy of our church, I made an impassioned speech arguing that for the church to decide on the issue of sexuality for gays and lesbians without consulting the psychiatrists and sociologists was like the church making a recommendation on the nature of the sun and moon without consulting the astronomers.

I touched off a heated debate by recommending that the insertion of the word "initially" be made after the words "be granted," which would make the report simply a provisional and temporary position of the church which could be changed later to support same-gender sexuality.[3] The vote on my amendment was so close we had to have a standing vote to count it, but it was defeated.

However, a time of great spiritual growth occurred over the next six years of my marriage, as my wife and I spent every weekday morning reading the Bible together, studying it, and having prayer. As we did, we both took the more literal view of Scripture on gays and lesbians, the view that was held by the Protestant and Roman Catholic denominations until about the middle of the twentieth century, against the approval of same-gender sexual relations. Since that time, God has not let me go,

21

and he has haunted me with the charge to "Rescue those being taken away to death, those who are staggering to the slaughter" (Proverbs 24:11).

The issue of homosexuality is not simply a social question. The words of Proverbs warn about the destruction and slaughter of those involved in all kinds of sexual immorality. Heterosexual sin is a behemoth the church must address, but if we make serious errors concerning homosexuality, we will lose our credibility and our ministry to announce God's will for *all* of sexuality. Our work to promote sexual purity and stable, traditional families will totally collapse, and our prophetic voice to address the nation will fall silent. When we fail to speak the mind of Christ faithfully on any aspect of morality, how can we ever recover the privilege, the credibility, and the integrity to speak, not just on sexual matters, but on the rest of the gospel? This book is my brief overture to answer that call from God.

When you walk into the Metropolitan Community Church in Toronto, which ministers to many in the GLBT community, you see these encompassing words from the prophet Isaiah spanning the front of the sanctuary: "For my house shall be called a house of prayer for all peoples" (Isaiah 55:7). The debate over the morality of homosexuality also demands an answer as to how we can include gays and lesbians in God's house of prayer.

The liberal element of the Christian church has pushed inclusiveness to the point of changing the traditional interpretation of Scripture and the historical practice of the church, urging us to approve of same-sex marriage, and gay and lesbian ordination, not merely as morally acceptable and equal, but even, in some aspects, as demonstrating exemplary Christian behavior.

This break with traditional Christian thinking has had an equal and opposite reaction from traditional, evangelical, orthodox Protestants and Roman Catholics who firmly reassert the historic interpretation of Scripture and tradition. Sometimes evangelicals become polemic, not recognizing or accepting the great advances for good that gays and their revisionist theologians have made to bring a persecuted and marginalized minority into full inclusion and participation in our contemporary world. While there may never be full agreement on the first and foremost issue of morality, evangelicals can and *must* find room to reconcile gays with the body of Christ on many significant, biblically supported levels.

In this book, I have attempted to present another way: neither the sharp disjunction gouging out the historic beliefs of traditional theology on the one side, nor on the other side, the knee-jerk reaction of bluntly and hurtfully condemning and criticizing gays and lesbians while barring them from any place in our world and consequently denying them any sense of self-worth. Hopefully this book will provide a new horizon, where the divisive war on this issue will move toward new levels of reconciliation and we can find acceptable terms of peace that gays and lesbians, and their ecclesiastical supporters, can acknowledge and live with.

Does Reinterpreting the Bible Make Peace?

How do we reconcile those with homosexual orientation with the historic body of Christ? What is our common ground? A powerful attempt to answer this question and "heal the church" has come from an esteemed moderator of the Presbyterian Church (USA) and a teacher at San Francisco Theological Seminary, Professor Jack Rogers. In his 2006 book *Jesus, the Bible, and Homosexuality: Explode the Myths, Heal the Church,* Professor Rogers seeks a breakthrough in biblical interpretation beyond "misused scripture" and "mythological interpretations" to "heal the church" from its intense division on the issue.[4] He does so, like a number of other scholars in prestigious seminaries, by seeking to revise the traditional interpretation of Scripture on homosexuality.

The main thesis of Rogers and other revisionist theologians like him is that biblical authors like Moses and St. Paul, as they wrote on the topic of homosexuality, did not understand gays and lesbians as we know them today—as faithful, believing, and committed couples who are not acting unnaturally, but exactly in the way God has made them to act. This present book will seek to answer what may appear to many readers as Professor Rogers' troubling hermeneutic, which does exactly the opposite of healing the church—it makes the debate even more intense.

The revisionist thrust at traditional theology using newly interpreted Scriptures has not presented us with what conservatives would like to see as terms of peace—it has actually represented more a declaration of war in the debate!

The truth is, the Bible need not be reinterpreted in order for us to find peace with those God loves. In these pages, as a conservative Christian thinker, I will seek to find common ground where, on the evangelical side, Christians can at the very least be civil and compassionate toward the GLBT community—and at the very best can bring forgiveness, unconditional love, and caring outreach to GLBT people, with the potential for changing lives. This book will also answer the question of whether same-sex sexual relations can ever be successfully read into Scripture in the passages revisionists cite as affirming homosexuality, or included under the broadest terms of justice and love—or whether the negative statements in references to homosexuality in the Bible are so indelibly present there that they can never be erased. The question of homosexuality and the church has a human quality to it. This debate will not come to an end even with conservative success in the interpretation of Scripture, because there are many important things we still need to talk about and agree upon in the church's ministry to homosexuals. As Andrew Marin says over and over in his book *Love Is an Orientation,* the church's answer to the GLBT community must not be a single closed answer, but very much an open-ended dialogue.[5] Conservative Christians may never be able to win over militant homosexuals, but many gays and lesbians are open to evangelical thinking, and some long for conservative Christian churches to help them live godly, biblical lives.

In this third paradigm of biblical faithfulness coupled with love and acceptance of gays and lesbians, some tough, unresolved moral and theological issues will need to be addressed. Nevertheless, the believing Christian church possesses all the right stuff in Scripture, and from a rational understanding of marriage in the natural world, to not only find an appropriate response to gays and lesbians, but also to achieve Isaiah's inclusiveness in God's house of prayer, offering healing and dignity to those who often are found to be hurting people.

The church will never be healed merely by a forced reinterpretation of Scripture, although some clergy accept the new hermeneutic, or by reinterpreting anything negative in the Bible about same-sex sexual relations into a kind of benign irrelevancy and believing the Bible has nothing to say about contemporary, loving, committed, Christian same-sex couples. The Christian Scriptures must be examined for positive examples of intimacy and sexual relations which God approves of, and although we may find a perplexing mix of sexual relationships revealed in various Scriptures, we must ask whether we can find a clear overall trajectory or positive pattern in the themes of God's plan for sexual relationships in Scripture as a whole.

There remain many potent issues in this debate, from simply longing to accept people as they are in a loving way, giving them equality and acceptance as normal people, to the more abstract philosophical analysis of the definition of marriage—but for all Christians, this debate will be finally lost or won according to the best, most accurate, and most comprehensive interpretation of Scripture, the quintessential authority for all branches of the body of Christ. If in this ecclesiastical debate we are to stop the divisiveness and public hemorrhaging of our faith, we must be very clear, convinced, and committed in our interpretation of Scripture.

The journey through Scripture over the next four chapters may be intense as we seek the most ethically compelling examples of intimacy and sexual relations in our search for God's revealed trajectory for sexual activity, but it is a necessary venture. Same-sex relations cannot be isolated from the wider and more inclusive issues involving all of human sexuality. Does God give a trajectory in the Bible for humankind's longing for sexual fulfillment? With that question, the search for the positive side of sexuality begins.

Chapter 2

OVERVIEW OF SEXUALITY IN THE BIBLE

C hurch documents and authors writing on homosexuality tend to address only the Scriptures that appear to speak negatively (or as some assert, "irrelevantly") to gay and lesbian sexuality. By contrast, we will start with the many positive things the Bible has to say about sexual relations in general. As the Presbyterian Church in Canada's initial study of homosexuality by the Committee on Church Doctrine reports:

> It should be noted that there are these texts that are all "negative," that is they all speak against a form of sexuality. There are "positive" passages which must also be considered, passages which speak of God's positive will for our sexuality…It would be a grave error in a study of human sexuality to focus only on passages which speak negatively of certain aspects of human sexuality.[6]

What does the Bible say about positive and affirmative intimacy and sexual relations, if anything at all?

THE CREATION PATTERN

The Bible has much to say on this topic! And in many, many places! Right from the beginning of the Bible, Adam, like the rest of all living beings, was made by God. Despite the presence of plant and animal life, there couldn't be found for Adam "a helper as his partner" (Genesis 2:20).

In response, God said, "It is not good that the man should be alone; I will make him a helper as his partner" (Genesis 2:18). God made a female partner, a "work mate" and a perfect companion for company in God's paradise. God commanded Adam and his female partner, like he did the rest of all living things, to "be fruitful and multiply" (Genesis 1:28). As the document from the PCC observes:

The description of the creation of the partner is followed by a reference to sexual union of the male and female partners... There is a strong tradition running through scripture that holds a positive view of sexual relations.[7]

God created humankind's first parents for the joy of sexual intercourse so as to be fruitful in bearing progeny. There may not be any mention of marriage in this creation account, but it is clear that God created man and woman to share sexual intercourse. The pattern of monogamous marriage emerges more and more over the centuries later in Scripture, but God sanctioned and designed man and woman to share sexual intimacy from the beginning. This is the first hint of a trajectory given by God in creation when "God saw everything that he had made, and indeed, it was very good" (Genesis 1:31). Here we can clearly see that God gave a woman to be man's companion for sexual intercourse, thus fulfilling their God-created potential "to be fruitful and multiply."

Throughout the stories of all the patriarchs, the prophets, the judges, the priests, the kings, and the everyday scoundrels and heroes of the Old Testament, God expanded the nation through sexual relationships. Often the believing Israelites copied the customs of their pagan neighbors around them and committed polygamy (Jacob), kept harems of wives and concubines (King Solomon), committed adultery (King David), practiced incest (Lot and his two daughters), prostituted themselves (Tamar with Judah), perpetrated gang rape (the tribe of Benjamin at Gibeah), or sought to have homosexual intercourse (the non-Israelites of Sodom and Gomorrah). These sexual relations were sometimes condemned, like David's adultery with Bathsheba and the incestuous rape of King David's daughter Tamar by his son Amnon. Some of these acts were openly censured by the prophets, and others were simply recorded without comment or ignored.

As the PCC observes:

Both Old and New Testament narrate misguided and, at times, calamitous sexual relations. Rape is a brutal form in which sin and lust are expressed (see, for example, Genesis 34, Deuteronomy 22:25–27, Judges 19:11–30, 2 Samuel 13). Adultery is another betrayal of God's intention for sexual fidelity in marriage. (See, for example, Deuteronomy 22:22–24, 2 Samuel 11, John 8:1–11.)[8]

The Old Testament is filled with a diverse and wide range of sexual practices. While none of these deviations from monogamy received God's revealed prophetic approval in the Old Testament, acceptance of the more positive patterns of intimacy in the Old Testament and positive, clear affirmations of patterns of sexual intimacy and marriage in the New Testament build toward a biblical trajectory highlighting that of which God does approve.

GOD'S GIFT OF SEXUAL UNION

The height of the celebration of sexual awakening in marriage is found in the Song of Songs, a poetic book in the Old Testament expressing the sexual desire of a virgin Israelite girl betrothed to her beloved fiancé (possibly King Solomon, as some think, or an unnamed ideal groom). This poetic love song shows God's approval of a man and woman's sexual love for each other, and it seems to foreshadow God's steadfast marital love for his bride, the church, made up of his believing community.

This reverence for marriage is also found in the biblical book of Esther, where a Jewish virgin named Hadassah married King Ahasuerus of Persia, and although he had other women in his harem, Esther became the queen and heroically saved her people from annihilation.

Although sexual intercourse appears frequently in most books of the Bible, no prophet declared sexual relations to be God's will with God's approval except where we find one man and one woman, as, for example, in the first glimpse of God's creation pattern of Adam and Eve. God saw their sexual complementary oneness and said it was "very good," revealing the beginning of an arch of monogamous, opposite-gender sexual unions in the Bible.

We earlier quoted the passage from Proverbs 2:16–19 in which a father warns his son against promiscuity and adultery. This same passage also issues a very positive statement on the proper sexual relations of a man with his wife, revealing the emerging pattern of the Bible's standard for approved sexuality:

> Drink water from your own cistern,
> flowing water from your own well.
> Should your springs be scattered abroad,
> streams of water in the streets?
> Let them be for yourself alone,
> and not for sharing with strangers.
> Let your fountain be blessed,
> and rejoice in the wife of your youth,
> a lovely deer, a graceful doe.
> May her breasts satisfy you at all times;
> may you be intoxicated always by her love.

PROVERBS 5:15–19

JESUS'S VIEW OF SEXUAL INTERCOURSE

Did the Lord Jesus Christ ever approve of sexual intercourse? Circumstantial evidence supports the idea that he did, as in his attending the wedding feast at Cana of Galilee and even performing his first great miracle there by turning water into wine. The Lord Jesus Christ also sanctioned man and woman in monogamous marriage when he answered a question about divorce by saying, "A man shall leave his father and mother and be joined to his wife, and the two shall become one flesh" (Mark 10:7–8). Thus Jesus gives the highest approval of God himself for a man and a woman enjoying the "oneness" of true marital union and sexual intercourse in marriage!

The apostles learned this lesson about sexuality within monogamous marriage from Jesus, as well as from each other, as shown when Paul asked in 1 Corinthians 9:5, "Don't I too also have the right to a believing wife?" Paul observed that the other apostles were "accompanied by a believing wife." The apostle Paul also exhorted the elders, deacons, and bishops seeking leadership in 1 Timothy 3:1–13 and Titus 1:5–9 to "be married only once" (or married to only one wife). Thus, where sexual unions are referred to in the New Testament, we find sanctioned sexual intercourse within a monogamous marriage of one man and one woman.

IS SEXUAL ATTRACTION EVER BAD?

Before looking at the documents to see whether homosexual sexual relations fit this emerging arch of approval, let us take a step backwards and examine sexual attraction, as opposed to sexually active relationships. Sexual attraction can be very different from sexual passion or lust, which result in sexual sin.

There is a general attraction—a longing for another person, a desire to be with him or her—and a more specific sexual attraction that arouses one's sexual feelings. Both are just part of our common human nature, whether we are attracted to the same sex or the opposite sex. Nowhere in the Christian Bible do we find condemnation of the innocent and pure longing for and even sexual feelings for someone, whatever their sexual orientation. God has made all of us, to varying degrees, to experience sexual attraction to others.

We can affirm this because sexual attraction can be innocent and without sin. However, sin does occur when sexual attraction becomes sexual fantasy, and a man, for example, "looks at a woman with lust" in his thoughts. Jesus said that such a man "has already committed adultery with her in his heart" (Matthew 5:28). When the attraction becomes lustful, sin enters in. And it is only when homosexuals' innocent and sinless attraction to the same sex becomes the "lusts of their hearts" (Romans 1:24) that God then gives them up to "degrading passions" (Romans 1:26).

Sexual attraction is common to us all, to some extent, and need not be considered sinful. I have been faithfully married for twenty-nine years. Early in my marriage I found I was becoming emotionally attracted to another married woman, and when I realized this, I stopped all occasions when we would be together alone. There was no fantasy, and there was no sin. I have always noticed a woman's beautiful face or figure, or her attractive hair, or her fashionable clothing, or elegant accessories like a tasteful necklace. And even though I have always been sexually attracted to the opposite sex, almost always that attraction has been without fantasies of lust or sexual passion. The same can be the experience of those with same-sex sexual attraction. It is not sin to feel this way, and it does not need to lead into sin.

How important for the church to accept that in some cases God has made gays and lesbians the way they are (although research shows homosexuality may also be a learned behavior[9]) so homosexuals can deal with the perplexing and anxious reality of being sexually attracted to the same sex! Attraction does not necessarily lead into sin. They can, with God's help and community support, live innocent and pure lives, even if it takes years of failures and successes to achieve this.

So often GLBT people talk about their crisis in accepting that they are different from most other people, possibly going through times of self-loathing or feeling that God has made a terrible mistake in making them this way. A story is told by Andrew Marin in *Love Is an Orientation*, his empathetic book on the GLBT community, about a woman who found Jesus Christ as her Lord and Savior as a teenager, but at the same time realized she sexually longed for other women. "I clearly did not realize," she writes, "that the next thirty years would be spent in a battle to gain a sense of purpose and value as a woman in the church."

At sixteen she began a sexual relationship with her best friend. Then, within months, she had a religious experience and came to a personal faith in Jesus Christ. As a reaction she, in a harsh way, tried to win others like her to Christ. Failing at this, she briefly threw herself into sexual relationships which later she deeply regretted.

Doing rounds of prayer, counseling, and "deliverance," her epiphany came when she encountered a lesbian friend at work who told her of a friend who had come out to her parents. She asked her friend how this confession went. "It went well," her friend told her, "because, you know, we all are born this way."

What this woman writes next is so important that I will quote it at length:

That night I went to God in prayer and gave him an ultimatum as I had for many years: "Lord, I am so tired of not having a response to someone who says that gays are born that way. I am not going to go another night without a response for them or for myself." I clearly heard in my spirit, "I created you perfectly, just as you are. How you walk out your journey regarding the totality of who you are will not take away from what I have already established and cherished in creating you."[10]

Whatever the mental or physical makeup with which we are born, God has made us all the way we are, including the diversity present between us and others. Some are born with a genetic predisposition to disease, or with a mental or physical disability, a disorder, or a physical disfigurement—but they are not mistakes of God. Although we can do much to work with and "correct" the mental and physical realities of the sick, the disabled, and the disfigured, or even of those with a disposition for same-gender orientation, and although we should never simply accept something that seems impossible to improve, we still must deal with the way God has made us. Christians should never criticize a condition that is difficult to change that doesn't lead to immoral activities. We must confess that God doesn't make mistakes in his creation of people—even though we may exhibit imperfections in our mental or genetic makeup.

But does acceptance of the way we are made mean that sexual orientation cannot and should not be changed? It can be noted from God's creation pattern found in Adam and Eve that men and women should have mental, physical, and emotional wholeness leading to sexual attraction for each other, which is consummated in their complementary oneness in sexual intercourse. Focus on the Family's website takes a wholesome view of this:

Focus on the Family is dedicated to defending the honor, dignity and value of the two sexes as created in God's image—intentionally made as male and female—each bringing unique and complementary qualities to sexuality and relationships.[11]

Evangelicals point out that God can heal disorders and disabilities, as we see happening in the Bible in the many miracles of Jesus, like the raising up of the lame and the blind. Evangelicals feel the same way about biological, genetic, or environmental disorders, like the demoniac with the disorder of mental illness that Jesus could and did heal. Should it be any different for sexuality?

Again, Focus on the Family has a very familiar definition of God's plan for sexual relations:

> God's created intent for sexual expression is limited to a monogamous, covenantal marriage relationship between a man and a woman.[12]

In agreement with many churches, Focus on the Family views homosexuality as a condition that God can heal. They positively and clearly affirm "the Scriptural teaching that homosexuals can and do change their sexual identity (1 Corinthians 6:9–11)" through a variety of restorative and supportive methods.[13] There are statistics showing that these therapies can lead men and women with same-sex attraction into successful chaste single lives or even into the positive relationship of the marriage of a man and a woman.[14] When we faithfully uphold the hope for God's plan for sexual relationships as revealed in humanity's progenitors, we help to motivate everyone toward healing and wholeness as revealed in the original creation pattern.

WHAT WE DO, NOT WHAT WE ARE

The determinative issue here is not the way God has made us mentally, physically, and emotionally, but what we do in our actions with our bodies. It is only by our actions that we are judged. If the United Church of Canada calls homosexuality "a gift from God,"[15] that can only apply to the bodily makeup that God has given us and not necessarily to the actions we freely choose that result in our doing moral or immoral deeds. While same-gender sexual activity may not be viewed, by some churches, as "a gift from God," the mental and physical bodies of the people participating in it can be. The same is true for persons who may have a disposition to alcoholism, addiction, promiscuity, adultery, or emotional or physical abuse. We are made by God, and God does not make mistakes. It is by our own freely chosen actions that we become either righteous or sinful and capable of enhancing or destroying God's good creation.

Sexual orientation is not sin, and it does not need to lead us into sin. And even when we, heterosexuals or homosexuals, do stumble and fall into sin, that does not change the fact that God made us, and we are still his creation. While much can be done today to help homosexuals change their orientation, even enabling some to achieve very successful heterosexual marriages, homosexuals who can't change—but have their bodies under control—can live very godly lives. And if we fall into sin—and that so often is not "if" but "when"—God has a plan in Jesus Christ to forgive us.

Experiencing a strong sexual attraction to the same gender or even having a history of experimenting sexually with others of the same sex does not mean individuals must give up any hope of leaving those things behind. With adequate restorative counseling and encouragement, and accountability from a support group such as you would find in some evangelical churches, there is great hope of reforming same-gender sexual attraction into a working opposite-gender orientation and even into the successful marriage of a man and a woman.[16]

Christians have a wonderful promise in Scripture: "If we confess our sins, he who is faithful and just will forgive us our sins and cleanse us from all unrighteousness" (1 John 1:9). The Lord Jesus Christ has made payment for all our sins at the cross, which anyone may receive freely to find God's gift of forgiveness, and with it, eternal life. At that moment of receiving forgiveness, we become more than a creation of God—we become children of God, a relationship which can, by the power of the Holy Spirit and in God's own timing, lead to repentance and newness of life.

Psalm 138:13–14 affirms the self-worth of us all, whoever we are, in whatever bodies God has placed us, from God's point of view as revealed to King David:

For it was you who formed my inward parts;
You knit me together in my mother's womb.
I praise you, for I am fearfully and wonderfully made.
Wonderful are your works;
That I know very well.

This Scripture applies to all of us. We should all realize that we are creations of God, and Christians especially should look at people and say, "You are one of us—a creation of a good and righteous God—and like us are in need of forgiveness."

INTRINSICALLY DISORDERED?

However, such acceptance can create its own confusions. It remains extremely perplexing for gays and lesbians to have Christians accept that they were created by God, and then for the same Christians to turn around and call them "an abomination" when they are only acting out on what God has made them to be. Again, the distinction here lies between what God has created us to be and the actions we freely choose to do. This principle applies whether we feel attraction to the opposite sex or the same sex. All humanity is a creation of an omnipotent God, and what's more, when we receive the Lord Jesus Christ as our personal Savior, each of us becomes a child of God, a son or daughter with Almighty God as our heavenly Father.

Christians in particular must always remember that we are offered help for self-control through the empowering presence of God's Holy Spirit. Sexual energy can be directed into all sorts of creative work, as witnessed in the vast majority of those celibates in religious orders who sublimate and channel their sexual energy into Christian ministry.

The Roman Catholic Church defined homosexuality in their 1995 and 1997 Catechism as "the relations between men or women who experience an exclusive or predominant sexual attraction toward persons of the same sex." Thus, even though a person may not be sexually active, he or she may have a homosexual orientation. However, we find the heart of the controversy between Catholics and homosexuals in the following text from that catechism:

> Basing itself on Sacred Scripture, which presents homosexual *acts* as *acts* of grave depravity, tradition has always declared that "homosexual *acts* are intrinsically disordered."[17] (*italics mine*)

These words have come down to gays and lesbians as highly critical and demeaning. This statement makes them feel, just because of the way they were made, that they are rejects by God, "intrinsically disordered," not part of God's good creation. But this term is only the description of specific *acts,* not a moral judgment on a person's orientation or feelings of attraction. It is not meant to demean and humiliate GLTB people but to identify the possible "disordered" actions of a condition.

Neither a gay priest nor a heterosexual priest who experiences sexual attraction sins if he does not look lustfully upon the person he is attracted to or dwell upon or act out a sexual fantasy. Both are equally innocent and pure and not in need of confession over the way God has made them. Both can rejoice that they are part of God's loving creation. This is true not just for Roman Catholic priests, but for ministers ordained in Protestant churches and for everyone.

Sexual attraction, for all of us, never needs to lead to evil. And even when we fail, as we so often do, to live according to God's original plan represented by humankind's first parents, it doesn't mean we can't accept ourselves or find forgiveness. We can get back on our feet with God's forgiveness and say, "God, you have made me this way; God, you are good, and I accept who I am. But I am sorry about what I have done and ask, dear God, for your forgiveness. I will try again to follow your plan."

The church should always be vigilant in defending, affirming, and protecting the self-worth of all of God's creation. God made us, despite our failures and sins, and destined a sinful world to receive forgiveness and healing in the Lord Jesus Christ, if we are willing to receive it.

Families Should Always Offer Steadfast Love

It must be said at this point that the family stands at an extremely important place for helping young men and women who experience same-gender attraction. Often, when the local congregation learns of the rebellion and experimentation of a gay or lesbian in their church, they withdraw from that person and his or her family and push them all away. The conservative preacher or scholar teaching on human sexuality from the Bible could push this gay person away by virtue of his teaching. Often, from early years in elementary school, the child who is effeminate or withdrawn from other boys in sports is bullied and rejected, so his school friends are taken away. And when that same gay man enters the workforce, fellow workers sometimes circulate secrets or surreptitiously tell antigay jokes that push the victim away into a lonely, painful life. What has happened? That young gay man has no supportive church where he can worship God, no Bible he can turn to, no understanding friends during his school years, and no supporters at work in the agony of rejection as an adult. What a scene for thoughts of ending your life! Such people have nothing left but their own gay community and the immense emptiness of being rejected by so many people.

Given this reality, it is tremendously important that the nuclear family remain supportive and accepting, while not necessarily approving. Mom and Dad may not agree with some of the things their children do, but it is vital that they remain firmly behind their son or daughter and show their unconditional, steadfast love. When this young gay man has everything taken away—his church, his Bible, his school friends, and his colleagues at work—his home must be a safe and supportive place so he can deal in a positive way with what makes him different.

The TV sitcom *The Cosby Show* had an episode where Clair Huxtable has a talk with her daughter about coming home and telling her she is pregnant. Clair declares she would kill her if she did this! But she hastens to add in a gentle and loving voice, "But we do above all else want you to come home and tell us! Remember, who loves you more than we do?"

Christian families must show their gay son or lesbian daughter unconditional love and support, even though they may not agree with their actions. Who, other than God himself, loves a child more than parents do? A parent's love and prayers can miraculously minister the saving grace of the Lord Jesus Christ to lead the child to heaven, and in God's own timing, to repentance. And the church home of that family should warmly welcome them and their gay son or daughter in a positive, supportive way. If the church pushes that family away, or even pushes away only the gay child, how will they find the life-supporting and life-changing gospel which alone has "the power of God for the salvation of everyone who believes" (Roman 1:16)?

A verse from the New Testament used over and over again on my national television program is John 3:16: "For God so loved the world." This should always convey huge self-esteem and self-acceptance to people everywhere. God has made us and loves us, if only we are willing to accept God's gift of a Savior and his forgiveness!

PORTRAITS OF SAME-SEX LOVE IN THE BIBLE

So far, our look at the Bible's trajectory for sexuality has highlighted monogamous marriage between a man and a woman. Does the Scripture have anything positive to say about other relationships? While we cannot find examples of approved same-gender *sexual* relationships, we do find portraits of great love between people of the same sex. The most outstanding example of this friendship love is between two princes: David, who was to become king of Israel, and the beloved son of the present king, Jonathan. They both were young men. Both were precariously at risk of death. They both were highly placed in the kingdom. And they both passionately loved the Lord God of Israel.

As Scripture records, Jonathan "loved [David] as his own soul" (1 Samuel 18:1), and again, "he loved [David] as his own life" (20:17). David also greatly loved Jonathan. After they made a covenant of mutual support, the Bible records:

> David arose [from hiding] and prostrated himself with his face
> to the ground. He bowed three times, and they kissed each

other, and wept with each other; David wept the more. Then Jonathan said to David, "Go in peace, since both of us have sworn in the name of the Lord, saying, 'The Lord shall be between me and you, and between my descendants and your descendants, forever.'"

1 SAMUEL 20:41–42

Later, when David learned that Jonathan and his father, King Saul, had died in battle, David immortalized his love for Jonathan in a psalm recorded in 2 Samuel 1:19–27:

Jonathan lies slain upon your high places.
I am distressed for you, my brother Jonathan;
greatly beloved were you to me;
your love to me was wonderful,
passing the love of women.

These men had so much in common in their deep friendship that despite what should have been deep political rivalry, they considered each other beloved brothers. We should also note that it is very common, even to this day, for men in the Middle East to kiss each other as a sign of greeting or friendship. While their friendship was greater than they found with others, there is not a hint or reference in any Scripture that David and Jonathan felt sexual desire for each other; even more remote is any hint of sexual intimacy. Both men were married and had children, and King David in his old age had a young virgin woman sleep with him in bed to keep him warm.

Another example of love and closeness in a same-sex relationship can be found in the love and respect Ruth had for her Jewish mother-in-law, Naomi. Naomi's husband had died, and both her married sons had died as well. She no longer had any future in Moab, a despised region outside Israel where she and her husband had migrated, so she prepared to return to her relatives in Bethlehem. Naomi bid farewell to her two daughters-in-law, but one of them, Ruth, so loved Naomi that she con-

fessed one of the most beautiful expressions of love in the entire Bible—
which, incidentally, is still often read at weddings today. Ruth vowed her
love to Naomi:

> Do not press me to leave you
> Or to turn back from following you!
> Where you go, I will go;
> Where you lodge, I will lodge;
> Your people shall be my people,
> And your God my God.
> Where you die, I will die—
> there will I be buried.
> May the Lord do thus and so with me,
> And more as well,
> If even death parts me from you!

Again, despite the beauty of this love poem, there is no hint to the
reader here, or in any other part of Scripture, that Naomi and Ruth had
any sexual attraction between them. This love poem expresses the bond
between two very loving relatives. And when they both returned to Bethlehem, Ruth fell in love with Boaz, a prosperous businessman. She married him, and they became the grandparents of King David.

JESUS AND SAME-SEX UNIONS

We have already seen that Jesus approved of sexual intercourse in the
monogamous marriage of a man and a woman at the wedding feast at
Cana of Galilee. Did Jesus support same-sex sexual relationships as well?
Is there a positive case for this in the New Testament?

Some revisionists think the New Testament offers Jesus's tacit
approval of sexual relations between same-gender partners because
Jesus did not say anything negative against homosexuals in the gospels.
Here I rely on the insights of an ex-gay minister, counselor, and leader
in the evangelical church in America, Joe Dallas, in his book, *The Gay
Gospel?*:

The idea, of course, is that if Jesus did not specifically forbid a behavior, then the behavior must not have been important to Him. Stretching the point further, this argument assumes that if Jesus was not manifestly concerned about something, we shouldn't be either.[18]

The further question arises that if not only Jesus, but the rest of the entire Bible, does not contain explicit negative references to "committed, faithful, Christian same-sex relationships," as we find in some of the gay and lesbian community today, why should the church be concerned to condemn committed homosexual unions today?

Reverend Dallas gives four reasons to explain the absence of any reference to homosexuality by Jesus.[19] The first reason is that we should not assume the gospels of Matthew, Mark, Luke, and John, which are the biographies of Jesus, to be more authoritative than other books in the Bible. Different books in the Bible bring different elements of faith to light through different material. Some prophecies in the Old Testament, like Isaiah and Jeremiah, have much more profound prose and poetry than other parts of the Bible, and some books, like Ezekiel, Daniel, and Revelation, contain much more future prophecy than other books. Different books offer different emphases, leading to the completeness of the Christian faith.

The Bible represents all of itself as inspired by the Holy Spirit, as Paul writes to his young colleague, Timothy, ministering in Ephesus:

All scripture is inspired by God and is useful for teaching, for reproof, for correction, and for training in righteousness.

2 TIMOTHY 3:16

Although not all books in the Bible comment on homosexuality, those that do are just as authoritative and inspired by the Holy Spirit as the gospels, despite the absence of Jesus's treatment of the topic in the gospels. And we will see in the next three chapters that although Jesus didn't condemn homosexuality explicitly in the gospels, many other passages in the Old and New Testament do, all of which are inspired by the Spirit of the Lord Jesus Christ. These passages too are part the inspired Word of God and help to fill out God's revealed will for sexuality.

Secondly, we must not assume that the gospels contain references to everything that is important to God. The gospels alone are not comprehensive of all that God has to say, or why would we need to be given the full canon of Scripture? The Lord Jesus Christ never addressed our current crises with gambling, addiction, alcoholism, or domestic abuse. Does this mean that these aren't important problems for the church, or to God, because Jesus never spoke about them? We can't condone current problems in North American culture just because Jesus didn't have anything to say about them in the gospels.

Thirdly, we can't presume to know everything Jesus said. The gospels are very brief books, having much content in common with each other. There just wasn't the technology or the real-life opportunity to record everything that Jesus said. In fact, at the end of the gospel of John, the apostle John says this very thing:

> But there are many other things that Jesus did; if every one of them were written down, I suppose that the world itself could not contain the books that would be written.

JOHN 21:25

If we don't have everything that Jesus said in the gospels, how do we know that he didn't address the topic of homosexuality at all?

Fourthly, the case for Jesus not explicitly condemning homosexuality wrongly assumes that he had nothing to say about heterosexuality as the standard for all sexual matters. As we have already seen, Jesus quoted God's inspired book of Genesis concerning sexual relations as between a man and a woman, thereby agreeing with the original creation pattern for sexual intimacy. The context for Jesus's quoting Genesis was a question by the Pharisees about marriage and divorce, which Jesus answered from the creation account of man and woman in Genesis 2:24:

For this reason a man shall leave his father and mother and be joined to his wife, and the two shall become one flesh. So they are no longer two, but one flesh.

Matthew 19:5–6

While Jesus may not have said anything in the gospels about homosexuality, he did most certainly define the monogamous marriage union of a man and a woman as the divine plan and revealed trajectory for marriage and sexual unions. Homosexuality may not be there, but Jesus's approval of monogamous heterosexuality certainly is!

The absence of Jesus's prohibition against homosexuality in the New Testament does not mean it is unimportant or without censure, because we do know most clearly that Jesus approved of heterosexual sexuality (and so too did the other biblical authors) to the exclusion of any other sexual unions.

What Are the Positive Views on Homosexuality in the Bible?

There remain three other references in the New Testament that pro-gay advocates point to as supporting their view that the Bible supports same-gender sexual relations.

First, in Matthew 8:5–13 and Luke 7:1–10, we find the moving account of a Roman centurion whose favorite "slave" (*pais* in Matthew and *doulos* in Luke) was gravely ill, possibly facing death. This soldier had done great good for the Jews, helping to build their synagogue, and appears to be a faithful believer in God. In fact, the man had such great faith and humility that he told the Lord not to bother himself by coming into his home, feeling he was unworthy to have such a great teacher and healer come into his house. "Lord," he said, "I am not worthy to have you come under my roof, but only speak the word, and my servant will be healed." Jesus, true to character, issued the word of healing, and immediately the slave got better. Matthew records, "When Jesus heard him, he was amazed and said to those who followed him, 'Truly, I tell you, in no one in Israel have I found such faith'" (Matthew 8:10).

Gay supporter Tom Horner here points out that the word for *slave* can mean a servant working for a master, or it can mean a weaker sexual partner.[20] However, *pais* or *doulos* do not have the latter meaning in literature inside the Bible, according to the *Harper Analytical Greek Lexicon*. The closest meaning to this for the word *doulos,* and a derivative form, *doulou,* occurs when it is "used figuratively, in a bad sense, meaning one involved in moral or spiritual thraldom" in four passages in the New Testament. It can mean "to be in bondage, spiritually or morally" in two other passages, according to this lexicon.[21] However, there is no specific word for, or reference to, homosexual activity in these passages.

Even if the centurion and his favorite slave were male sexual partners, I have no doubt that Jesus would go to help them as Jesus always did for people with all kinds of different needs. But after visiting the two men and healing the sick slave, it seems highly unlikely the Lord Jesus Christ would leave without saying to them exactly what he said to the Samaritan woman in John 4:7–42, to the woman taken in adultery in John 7:53–8:11, and to Zacchaeus (Luke 19:1–10): "Go and sin no more." These words commanding repentance and forgiveness stand completely consistent with the historical Jesus we find throughout the New Testament. We would realistically expect Jesus to say "sin no more" in this context to a homosexually active centurion as well.

Nevertheless, the liberal says the word *pais* or *doulos* likely means that this favorite slave was a lover of the centurion, thus accounting for his love in having him healed. When Jesus heals the slave and commends the man's faith, they conclude that Jesus is giving tacit support to a homosexual relationship. But the argument doesn't hold up. Even if this were a homosexual relationship, Jesus healed a man because of Jesus's grace and mercy, not because the slave morally earned this grace of healing. Also, Jesus commended the centurion's faith, not his moral conduct.

A parallel to commending faith but not conduct can be found in the hall of the biblical heroes in the book of Hebrews in the New Testament, where we find the name of the prostitute Rahab, who helped the Israelite spies in Jericho, as found in Joshua 2:1–24. Although the Bible does not approve of prostitution, she is commended in the list of the saints in Hebrews 11:31: "By faith Rahab the prostitute did not perish with those who were disobedient, because she had received the spies in peace." This passage shows that it was the prostitute's faith, not her immoral actions, that the Bible approves of.

Jesus's healing does not mean Jesus approved of their actions even if they were homosexuals, any more than Rahab was commended for her prostitution. Both Rahab and the centurion are commended because they both had great faith. Jesus gives no tacit approval of the actions of the centurion, only his great faith. It also seems highly unlikely that the Jews would hold this man in such high esteem if he were a practicing homosexual, commending him as a friend of their nation and supporter of their faith.

THE EUNUCH'S EVERLASTING NAME

The second passage in question is the one where Jesus speaks positively about eunuchs, which Tom Horner infers as approval of homosexuals.[22] Jesus, when pressed by the Pharisees to answers questions on divorce, gave a very strict teaching on lifelong marriage, shocking his disciples so much that they said it would be better not to marry at all. Jesus replied to their statement on not marrying:

> Not everyone can accept this teaching, but only those to whom
> it is given. For there are eunuchs who have been so from birth,
> and there are eunuchs who have been made eunuchs by others,
> and there are eunuchs who have made themselves eunuchs for
> the sake of the kingdom of heaven.
>
> MATTHEW 19:12

The gay advocate interprets this to mean that the homosexual is born unable to have sexual relations with a woman, and this is what Jesus refers to as "eunuchs who have been so from birth." This passage is then combined with Isaiah 56:4–5, which says:

> For thus says the Lord: To the eunuchs who keep my Sabbaths,
> who choose the things that please me and hold fast my

covenant, I will give in my house and within my walls, a monument and a name better than sons or daughters; I will give them an everlasting name that shall not be cut off.

The revisionist now concludes that the Bible accepts and affirms the homosexual as the eunuch who is despised and rejected by humankind, but upheld and honored by God. Thus the revisionists argue that Jesus is here speaking positively of the dispossessed and disenfranchised homosexuals ("born eunuchs"), especially when taken along with the Isaiah 56:4–5 passage above, affirming them and legitimizing their active sexuality.

But is this interpretation fair to the text? Briefly, the Hebrew word used everywhere where the word *eunuch* appears in the Bible is *cariyc*. It comes from the root word meaning "to castrate."

From birth, some boys would be prepared for work in the king's palace, and especially around his harem, by castration that mutilated the sex organs and so rendered them sexually harmless in the king's service—they could neither pose a danger to his wives nor give birth to children who would represent a competing interest to their loyalty. Even in the Renaissance and Baroque periods, in music, the *castrati* from birth would be prepared for the falsetto parts in choral music in the great concert halls of Europe. They were the eunuchs made so by man. To be either born without functional sexual organs or to be castrated by men is the biblical meaning of *eunuch*—without any reference to homosexuals, who can often function very well with those of their own orientation.

The compassion of the Lord God of Israel revealed in the Isaiah passage for eunuchs is the same grace and mercy that the Lord Jesus spoke of in the Sermon on the Mount when he said, "Blessed are the meek, for they shall inherit the kingdom of God." The tender love of God for eunuchs does not constitute approval of homosexuals. Rather, it declares that all men who are completely unable to have any sexual functioning will, by faithful observance of God's law, receive "an everlasting name."

And the eunuchs "who have made themselves eunuchs for the sake of the kingdom of heaven" (Matthew 19:12) are those disciples who freely choose a life of sexual continence for the sake of giving complete service and devotion to the Lord in the same way as the castrated eunuch does to his king in the service of the palace harem.

THE DISCIPLE JESUS LOVED

There are several references in the apostle John's biography of Jesus to the "disciple that Jesus loved" (John 13:23 and John 21:20). A wall mural in Italy has forever etched the world's portrait of Jesus and "the disciple Jesus loved" together at the Last Supper in the wall fresco painted by Leonardo da Vinci. There we see a very effeminate and young John ("the one Jesus loved") leaning on the shoulder of his Master.

Dan Brown, in his popular book *The Da Vinci Code,* goes as far as identifying this "beautiful" John as in reality being Mary Magdalene, whom he would like to think of as Jesus's lover. The Bible makes it clear that at the Last Supper, it was indeed John, "the disciple Jesus loved," leaning on Jesus's shoulder. But the love between Jesus and John has never been viewed in the Bible or in all of Christian history as homosexual love. Jesus would be in his midthirties at this point in his ministry, and John would probably still be a teenager. It is common for a younger man to love his mentor, and likewise the mentor his protégé.

Just like we found in the love between David and Jonathan, nonsexual love between friends has been accepted and normal throughout history. Moreover, even in our own time and culture, it is not uncommon to see fathers, because of their love, kiss their sons, and on some occasions not just as children but also as adults.

Jesus loved the disciple John, just as Jesus loved Mary and her sister Martha and their brother Lazarus, and as he loved the rich young ruler who lived such a moral life and asked Jesus how to inherit eternal life (Mark 10:17–22). None of these ever demonstrated sexual passion or sexual immortality.

Jesus and the disciple John do not affirm or legitimize homosexuality, because their love is exactly like the love that both men and women have for the Lord Jesus Christ today. Often in worship we sing the praise song "As a Deer," where both men and women sing to the Lord Jesus Christ about how we love him more than any other. Just like the apostle John, so do Christians today love the Lord Jesus Christ above all else.

To conclude: Jesus did approve of opposite-sex monogamy in the gospels, in concert with many other places throughout the Bible that approve of such unions, but we have not yet found a passage or story where same-gender sexual relations are approved of. This begins to sketch a biblical trajectory for divinely approved sexual relationships between people.

In the next three chapters, we will look at specific texts on homosexual relations. A report on homosexuality by the Church Doctrine Committee of the Presbyterian Church in Canada makes this observation:

> It cannot be said that the Bible very often speaks of homosexual practices but where it does it speaks of them with disfavor. On the other hand it frequently celebrates the joys of committed heterosexuality. Its voice with respect to homosexual practices is, therefore, quite clear and consistent, in fact unusually so. We cannot find any hermeneutical principle which will allow us to ignore this clear word. Nor does any general theological approach to scripture which emphasizes love, or liberation to the exclusion of the demand of holiness commend itself to our approval.[23]

Having seen the positive portrait in the Scriptures of God's plan for sexuality and the preliminary scriptural trajectory for sexual unions for heterosexuals, how do we interpret what Scripture does say about homosexuality? Homosexuality does appear in the Bible. Does Scripture speak only negatively on homosexuality, or can these negative references be explained away with a better interpretation? What does the current debate in the church over Scripture tell us about the morality of same-sex unions?

The revisionists who are calling for change in the interpretation of Scripture know how crucial it is for them to find support from Scripture in this debate on homosexuality. They know that support from Scripture has always been and will continue to be the litmus test for any legitimate change in the church, and that they must clear the way through the Bible if they want to change the church's policy. Hence revisionism. But how do they fare at this? In the next three chapters, we will carefully consider Scripture as it is quoted and interpreted in two documents on homosexuality that at first appear very similar but that lead us into two very different outcomes. Where will the best and most comprehensive view of Scripture lead us?

Chapter 3

Homosexuality in the Old Testament: Battling a Giant

D espite compelling emotional reasons and societal pressures to embrace homosexual lifestyles, the conservative side of the Christian church remains adamantly opposed to same-sex sexual relations. Why? There are several reasons, but at the heart of the matter lies what the conservative churches find to be the most clear and compelling interpretation of Scripture and the continuing reality of their living within the culture of the biblical world.

In this chapter, we will compare the left and the right sides of the issue by looking at the interpretation of Old Testament Scripture in two very similar documents with two very different results. Both of these opposing giants use Scripture to clinch their case. We will study both sides in our search for the most convincing interpretation of God's Word.

The first is *Jesus, the Bible, and Homosexuality,* the scholarly presentation by a leading churchman from the Presbyterian Church (USA), Professor Jack Rogers, who has taken a new look at giving full rights to the gay community. The second is *Reports on Sexuality,* a similar study by the Presbyterian Church in Canada (PCC), which reflects a more traditional position by a Christian denomination not unlike the Presbyterian Church (USA), of which Professor Rogers has served at the highest level as moderator. The documents from the PCC came early in the debate over homosexuality and the church, but they reflect a very thoughtful and biblical position that doesn't need to be reinvented.

Both of these documents are North American; both are Presbyterian; both deal with the same Scriptures; both are highly esteemed and accepted by many—and both offer completely different results!

Professor Rogers has changed his mind about homosexuals. "I have gone through a change in my mind and heart," he writes in *Jesus, the Bible, and Homosexuality.*

> I have gone from being a silent spectator to actively working for change. I believe people who are homosexual should be given full rights of membership in the church and citizenship in the nation. I believe that this is the only way to heal the wounds of the church and the nation.[24]

By "full rights in membership in the church," he invites gays and lesbians not only to participate in every activity in the church, but also supports them in having full opportunity for ordination and leadership at every level of the denomination. By "rights of citizenship," he means full acceptance and equality in marriage and adoption of children, with the same rights and benefits as are given to married heterosexuals.

Professor Rogers writes a very impassioned appeal for the church to open our hearts and doors to a misunderstood minority that the church has oppressed in a history of intentional and hurtful "misinterpretation of scripture." He proceeds to explode the church's deliberate misuse of "the Bible to justify oppression."

Rogers' book not only offers a scholarly study on the history of the church's pattern of resistance to abolition, divorce, the equality of women, and a detailed review of foundational documents for interpreting the Bible, but also tells a very personal story of his encounter with and love for members of the GLBT community over the years. The reader can see a professor's passion and a pastor's heart in his book with its many insights and compelling arguments.

However, Professor Rogers does not seem to recognize the painful dilemma and inevitable conflict his hermeneutics of the Bible passages on homosexuality cause for the conservative, believing church. While his goals can be accepted by some in the church, there remain huge roadblocks for others.

Even though this debate calls for the use of Scripture, tradition, reason, and experience, the paramount source and final authority among

Christian denominations has always been Scripture. The Christian churches possess a treasure of great minds serving in great universities, but if the church speaks, it cannot be from the mind of any one person or any prestigious school. Rather, as the PCC clearly testifies, it must speak with the authority of the recognized norm for all churches, including Reformed churches, around the world:

> The ultimate authority for the Church and for Christian faith and life is God, revealed in Jesus Christ, witnessed to by the Holy Spirit speaking to the Church in the Scriptures.[25]

Our discussion on homosexuality attempts to follow the example of the apostle Paul in his letter to the Ephesians, c. 52–53 AD. As in so many of the cities where the first apostolic churches were founded, in Ephesus some lived immoral lives or taught false doctrine. Paul passionately wanted the church to remain faithful to the original gospel message he had proclaimed to them, as he wrote:

> We must no longer be children, tossed to and fro and blown about by every wind of doctrine, by people's trickery, by their craftiness in deceitful scheming. But *speaking the truth in love,* we must grow up into him who is the head, into Christ.

EPHESIANS 4:14–15, *ITALICS MINE*

Christians are commanded to love people. Especially in proclaiming the gospel to the GLBT community, this means not only offering a ministry of compassion, pastoral care, and support, but with love and pastoral care having the courage to speak "the truth in love," as Paul commanded the Ephesians to do.

In our sexually antinomian culture, to tell the world about God's will on sexual matters (which the world may very much be interested to hear, although likely uninterested to obey) and what God has said about sexual relationships requires sensitivity, love, and courage. The world does not just want Christian sympathy or love; everyone, including the GLBT community, wants to know *the truth!* We must "speak the truth in love" from the clearest and most compelling sense of God's Word in Scripture.

For almost all of the last half-year, I have taken time out from writing this book and quietly reflected on the new hermeneutic in the reinterpretation of Scripture that supports gay marriage and ordination, and I have been rereading prayerfully the various passages on homosexuality, and sexuality generally, in different translations of the Bible. I prayerfully submit the following interpretation of the Scriptures, with the support of the other evangelical Bible interpreters I have used, which I believe are clearly and authoritatively given to Christians, and through them, to the audience of the world. We will bring the interpretations of Professor Rogers and the PCC to bear as we journey through these passages as well.

SODOM AND GOMORRAH

The first occurrence of homosexuality in the Bible comes on stage in the story of Sodom and Gomorrah in Genesis 18 and 19. The Lord appears in human form, along with two angels also in human form, before Abraham by the oaks of Mamre, not far from the valley cities of Sodom and Gomorrah. The Lord has come to announce to Abraham and his wife Sarah that in their old age they will have a son of promise.

At the same time, the Lord has also come because of the "great outcry against Sodom and Gomorrah and how very grave their sin is" (Genesis 18:20), a report that has even reached the Lord in heaven. "I must go down," the Lord tells Abraham, "and see whether they have done altogether according to the outcry that has come to me." (18:21).

Not able to find even ten righteous men to spare God's judgment on Sodom, the two angels of the Lord arrive in Sodom about nightfall and take lodging in the home of Lot, who insists they stay with him according to the strong custom of ancient Middle Eastern hospitality.

Now the plot thickens: "The men of Sodom, both young and old, all the people to the last man, surrounded the house" (19:4). The Bible continues: "They called to Lot, 'Where are the men who came to you tonight? Bring them out to us, so that we may know them'" (19:5).

What is clear is that a group of men, and only men, call for two strangers, both in the appearance of men, to come before them, that these men of Sodom may "know them."

"To know" someone in the Bible is a euphemism for carnal knowledge or sexual intercourse. Most people can recall the King James Version of the Bible read on Christmas Eve when the angel Gabriel announces to Mary that she will conceive and bear a son. It is correctly translated from the Greek in the King James Bible when Mary replies to the angel, "How shall this be, seeing I know not a man?" (Luke 1:34). Mary had never known sexual intercourse, the meaning of the term "to know."

The men of Sodom want to have carnal knowledge or sexual intercourse ("to know") with the two male visitors sheltered in Lot's house. Lot appears to perceive their desire for sexual relations and offers his two daughters in the men's place: "I beg you, my brothers, do not act so wickedly. Look, I have two daughters who have not known a man" (another reference to his daughters not having had sexual intercourse). "Let me bring them out to you, and do to them as you please" (19:7). Here the men of Sodom are offered sexual intercourse, not with the two male visitors, but with Lot's two daughters—an offer which the men of Sodom reject. They continue their violent advance against Lot for "judging" (19:9) their behavior.

Besides the homosexual acts of men with men, there are two other issues here: first, the crime against Middle Eastern hospitality, which seeks to save the two male visitors from violence and possible rape; second, the sheer violence of the men of Sodom in threatening to attack the visitors with possible sexual assault, or worse, murder.

Professor Jack Rogers writes that Sodom offends against the imperative of eastern hospitality, "where [the sin is that] foreigners are clearly not welcome, and the implication is that they may be raped or killed."[26] Rogers quotes scholars to argue that this rape is not homosexual acts as we know them today, but acts in the ancient world "for victors to accentuate the subjection of captive enemies and foes."[27] However, Rogers' reference to "sexual penetration to humiliate an enemy" is an obscure idea with no relevance to any passage in the Christian Scriptures.

Rogers also points out that to offer his two daughters, Lot did not "think of the attackers as primarily homosexuals or he would not have offered women for them to abuse."[28] But the men of Sodom rejected Lot's offer of his two virgin daughters, continuing their pursuit against Lot and his two male visitors.

Rogers presents a summary statement for Sodom and Gomorrah: "The best available scholarship shows that these texts have nothing to do with homosexuality as such."[29]

While the elements of offending ancient hospitality and the threat of injustice and murderous violence are found within the story of Sodom, nevertheless the threat of male sexual relations with men (homosexual acts) is indelibly written into this story and cannot be completely erased from the text. A very real part of God's judgment on Sodom and Gomorrah comes not just from their violation of eastern hospitality, injustice, murderous violence, and possible gang rape, but the sexual advance of men seeking sex with other men. All these elements are undeniably present.

The sins of Sodom are referred to in other books of the Bible, such as elsewhere in Genesis, Deuteronomy, Isaiah, Jeremiah, Lamentations, Ezekiel, Amos, Zephaniah, Matthew, Luke, Romans, 2 Peter, Jude, Revelation, and two intertestamental books.[30] Often the reference isn't to sexual sins, but to "greed, injustice, inhospitality, excess wealth, indifference to the poor, and general wickedness,"[31] as listed by Professor Rogers. But references are also made to Sodom's sexual sin in Ezekiel 16:44–58 and in 2 Peter 2:6–10, where Peter writes:

> By turning the cities of Sodom and Gomorrah to ashes he condemned them to extinction…then the Lord knows how to rescue the godly from trials, and to keep the unrighteous under punishment until the day of judgment, and especially those who indulge in the lust of defiling passion and despise authority.
>
> 2 PETER 2:6, 9–10

Same-sex intercourse is clearly implied in this passage and is at least one element in God's punishment of Sodom.

Where else do we find authoritative Scripture teaching that homosexual acts are in themselves wrong, helping to explain the judgment of Sodom? What more does Old Testament Scripture say about the acts that brought the destruction of Sodom and Gomorrah?

MOSES'S CONTRIBUTION TO THE DEBATE

Moses's direct words come next, addressing homosexuality and passing judgment on its moral value. Moses was a prophet of Yahweh, the God of the Israelites, and was called by God to deliver the Jewish slaves in Egypt from their captors. He led them across the desert of the Sinai Peninsula toward the promised land of Canaan.

As the Israelites left the pagan religion of Egypt and faced the impure cultic practices of the Canaanites in the land where they were going, they needed to be led by God to find their own forms of worship, religious practices, and moral codes to preserve what God had revealed to them and foster their separate religious identity. What resulted was the liturgical and legal third book of the Torah, called Leviticus, within which we find what is sometimes called "the Holiness Code." This phrase gets its name from a recurring verse in Leviticus: "You shall be holy, for I the Lord your God am holy" (Leviticus 19:2).

Within that code, we find these two references to homosexuality: Leviticus 18:22, "You shall not lie with a male as with a woman," and Leviticus 20:13, "If a man lies with a male as with a woman, both of them have committed an abomination; they shall be put to death; their blood is upon them."

The most obvious and clear meaning to the reader is that God revealed to Moses that homosexual sexual relations are morally unacceptable. This has been the traditional interpretation of Leviticus from the beginning up to our own time. Moses, "the friend of God," stood close to God to prophetically lead Israel and be the vehicle through which God conveyed the Torah, the law, to God's chosen people. No confusion or ambiguity has arisen from these two verses for Bible interpreters for over three and a half millennia. Yet today, in the emancipation of homosexuals from obscurity and secret lives, these passages in Scripture are being reexamined and revised.

Some Bible interpreters today see the immense change in culture from Moses's time to our own, where homosexuals today practice their faith within the believing community and want to share in Christian marriage just like heterosexuals. How do these scholars interpret Leviticus in light of this?

The answer for them resides in viewing Leviticus as a foreign culture different from what we know of the church and homosexuals today. Professor Rogers writes that the Israelites "needed cohesiveness, cleanliness and order in every aspect of their lives...Failure to form a tightknit community could threaten their long-term survival. They needed a code for living."[32]

Rogers needs to remember that the churches still do, and always will, need a code, positive guidelines for living, to help people make the right moral choices. That aside, Rogers argues that Moses and the Jewish people had to find cultic practices and beliefs that were relevant for their time in history and for the cultural demands they faced. Rogers observes three distinct developments:

- Israel's worship practices had to be different.
- Israel could not mix with foreigners, marry foreigners, nor mix the sowing of grains, nor mix the types of cloth in a garment—they had to have purity.
- Male superiority must be maintained and mixing gender identities, such as in homosexual relationships, was impure and must be prohibited.[33]

In this regard, there is a significant sentence in Rogers' book that I will take time to discuss at length. It reveals the huge gulf between the culture of the conservative, orthodox believing scholar and the revisionist teacher, shown by Rogers' attempt to reinterpret the relevance of the "Holiness Code" for us today. Rogers writes:

They [the Israelites] needed a code for living. In response, *they developed* a Holiness Code to define their religious, civic, and cultural identity. The Holiness Code's function was to achieve the "holy purity" *they* sought.[34] (*italics mine*)

Rogers claims that it was Moses and the Jews who thought through their needs as "they developed" and wrote the Holiness Code. This is a hallmark statement of the liberal church. They see man as the subject who writes Scripture, that Moses himself "developed" the Holiness Code as man's creation.

While Rogers believes Moses created the Holiness Code, many other scholars would still look to the repeated refrain throughout Leviticus that states: "The Lord spoke to Moses, saying..." (Leviticus 1:1; 4:1; 5:14; 6:1; 6:8; 6:19; 6:24; 7:22; 7:28; 8:1, etc.). Almost at the beginning of every chapter of Leviticus, this statement of God's speaking directly to Moses reoccurs. For scholars who accept the truth of those words, the Holiness Code belongs to what "the Lord spoke to Moses" and not to what Moses sought to create for Israelite culture, religion, and purity.

Rogers and other revisionist scholars credit Moses and Israel with the creation of a code that ensured their religious and cultural purity— and if this is man's creation, then it can be changed in our own day by man, when the leadership changes after Moses or the culture changes after this time in history. All this is possible if Moses and the Israelites constructed their own Holiness Code as a man-made thing.

Rogers identifies Moses's Scripture as being unique to its time, place, and people, and sees the code as a cultural adjustment and adaptation relevant only within that context. Thus the code can be reinterpreted as commandments only for Israel then, without having any enduring relevance. There is much more than a reinterpretation of Scripture at stake here. As we struggle to understand why this issue has become so divisive in the church, we need to carefully note the enormous cultural differences between liberal Christians and those who are more evangelical.

For the moment, let us make a significant departure from the study of Scripture and explore the underlying cultures of both the liberals and the conservatives in the church, cultures that support, shape, and drive their different interpretations of Scripture and their resultant theologies.

WHICH CULTURE DO WE LIVE IN?

We may all share the same geography, but the Christian pro-gay advocate lives in a very different world from that of the conservative Christian scholar. Pro-gay Christians define their world by the secular universities of our time and by the mass media of the press, television, radio, and cinema, where almost all insights come from science and mass culture, and where truth can be discovered without any need for any absolute revelation from God, whether in the Bible or elsewhere. For many Christian adherents to secular culture, miracles have little to do with an interactive God working directly in the natural world; they are just unusual, often wonderful, events in the natural world. Thus some leaders of these revisionist churches can deny the more inexplicable miracles in the Bible, like the virgin birth (Luke 1:26–38),[35] the bodily resurrection of the Lord Jesus Christ (John 20:1–31),[36] and the crossing of the Red Sea by Moses and Israel during the exodus (Exodus 14:1–31).[37]

This secular culture is the very air the revisionist breathes, almost unconsciously. It is everywhere because it is the culture of mass society. All of us, whatever our beliefs, inhale this mass culture every day, from everywhere around us.

One of Canada's best New Testament scholars and newspaper journalists, Tom Harpur, has lost his evangelical faith because, as he has said, evangelical believers can try to stay at the bottom of a lake with their precious biblical faith, but after a while they must come up to the surface for air where the world lives. He only found air to breathe in the unbelieving, secular world. And it is this culture that the revisionist brings to the interpretation of Scripture, holding various degrees of faith.

Frequently the revisionist knows very little about why the evangelical is so intractable in his beliefs, often attributing the evangelical use of Scripture to unthinking literalism. However, the orthodox believer's faith comes from the very biblical world in which such believers live and think. Orthodox scholars actually live and hold their beliefs within the same cultural world as those who wrote the Scriptures—they share the same interior beliefs in the Bible's miracles; the same consensus of faith found within Scripture in understanding God's nature; the same morality as found there; the same pattern of family life with mothers and fathers raising obedient, believing children and fathers as servant leaders committed to leading their families and "giving up their lives for their wives as Christ did for the church" (Ephesians 5:25).

Conservative Christians have seen the same need Moses did—to preserve the faith by marrying within the faith; to defend the faith against the influence of a foreign, unbelieving world; and to live a holy life despite the influence of the surrounding fallen cultures. Much of Moses's Holiness Code is the Holiness Code of evangelicals in today's world, including the moral teaching on homosexuality. In a moment, we will see why some commands and penalties within the code are no longer in effect. But the conservative Christian sees a significant continuity of culture between Moses's time and our own.

THIRD WORLD—LIKE OUR OWN WORLD?

There is on my desk a glossy magazine published by a Christian mission called Gospel for Asia. They minister the gospel to peoples in the 10:40 window, which includes the least-reached people groups in the world. They have Bible colleges, missionaries, and evangelists who serve in the developing world where the technology and communal living are much like the world we read of in the book of the Acts.

Their missionaries live on a dollar a day. They often walk the roads to evangelize, just as Paul and Silas did. They pray for the sick and record answered prayers where the blind receive their sight, the lame walk, the lost receive their miracle of salvation, and demons are cast out of tormented people, even giving reports of the dead being raised again and the multiplication of food to feed crowds.[38] (For identical miracles of Jesus, see Matthew 4:23–25). Gospel for Asia operates in the same cultural world we read about in the stories of the prophets of the Old Testament and the mission of Jesus and the apostles in the New Testament. It is all the same world as found in the Bible.

So what about the culture of conservative Christians and scholars today in the USA, Europe, and Canada? The Gospel for Asia magazine, in full color with digital photography and professionally written stories and testimonies, receives prayers, financial support, and a sense of common spiritual identity from Christians in the most developed parts of the world. Third World, First World, and biblical world all converge for many evangelicals in our reading of the Scriptures.

Often, the contrast between the conservative and revisionist Christian has been summarized by the terms "Bible-believing worldview" and "secular worldview." Both live in the same country, but one is immersed and influenced by the surrounding mass secular culture and its worldview, while the other lives "in" the same world but is not "of" it, living instead in the same culture as found in the Bible and the missionary world of a ministry like Gospel for Asia.

What happens when the culture of the ancient world changes over time? In that situation, changes in culture require a very careful Christian critique to examine whether or not they are within the parameters of Scripture. For Christians, cultural change can only be truly analyzed from the clearest and most compelling understanding of Scripture. Changes to institutions like slavery or the subjugation and marginalization of woman are important and valuable to conservatives, yet they reject most of the cultural shift we have seen in the "sexual revolution" and our present-day "culture of drugs."

Homosexuality: The Slavery Issue of Our Time?

Professor Rogers has researched extensively how the Presbyterian Church has changed its mind on significant moral issues such as slavery, segregation, the role of women in the church and society, and divorce. He sees prejudice against the equality of homosexuals as another issue that will change, as he himself did. Rogers writes:

> Homosexuality is not the first social issue with which the Presbyterian Church has wrestled that evokes high emotion. There have been many issues that, at the time, seemed to threaten the unity, indeed the very existence, of the church.[39]

It must be recognized that there has been a significant cultural change in Europe and North America regarding the moral equality of gays and lesbians with heterosexuals. Our North American culture is redolent with praise from equal rights supporters for full equality for gays and lesbians—it's heard on talk shows, every newscast, most television shows, movies, and from almost every media personality.

The media tells us that they see the emancipation of homosexuals as the "slavery issue" of our time. Rogers sees this cultural shift as being just like other moral issues which the church has faced and resisted. The subtitle of his book, *Explode the Myths, Heal the Church,* declares Rogers' fervent desire to accept the full equal rights of the GLBT community— an issue just like all the others where the church, liberal and conservative alike, has changed its mind in the past.

But there is a massive difference between this issue and those of the past that Rogers chooses to overlook. Yes, the liberal and conservative churches have changed together on views of slavery and segregation and a few other issues, but the orthodox, believing scholar can only make these changes if they find support in Scripture. There must always be confirmation from Scripture to support any cultural change. Scripture's authority must be there to justify changes because the God revealed in Scripture "does not change" (Malachi 3:6): as recorded in Hebrews 13:8, "Jesus Christ the same yesterday, today and forever."

Our God and the words that God speaks in Scripture just do not change. When God revealed the injunction against homosexuality to Moses in the Holiness Code of Leviticus, God was not just speaking to the needs of Moses's time and place. God could see the expanse of culture for all times and places in the future as well. The God revealed in the cultural settings of the Old and New Testaments, the commands and nature of this God, are enduring and unchanging, requiring cautious and reverent analysis to discern any legitimate shifts in our understanding of God's will. An international guest on my television program, *Reachout for Life,* Dr. T.V. Thomas, found as a young scholar that the Bible never needed to be revised, unlike so many writings of great thinkers over the years. In fact, this helped Dr. Thomas see the authority of Scripture that led him to become a Christian.

The Christian churches accepted the emancipation of slaves and the equal rights of women due to understanding the true meaning of Scripture, not by any departure from what was there or acceptance of what was not there. In these examples, it was not that Scripture was wrong, but that man's prejudiced views and interpretations were.

Take, for example, the ordination of women, a practice now fully accepted by most mainline Protestant denominations in North America. Southern Baptists, another major Christian denomination, do not accept the ordination of women, but some Baptist ministers I have talked to recognize that Presbyterians have a number of passages in Scripture supporting their policy. The Baptists see the case for ordaining women as much weaker than their own, but they must accept that there are a number of significant passages in Scripture supporting women in ministry.

If the Scriptures used by Presbyterians to support women clergy were not there, and worse yet, if all the references to women's ordination were negative, the church would be in a crisis with its constituency, possibly touching off a revolution, in choosing to ordain women. While this just isn't the case for female ministers, it is now exactly the case for evangelicals who view the marriage and ordination of homosexuals in the light of the lack of support from Scripture.

Change cannot be made by revising and reinterpreting Scripture alone, unless Scripture allows for this within itself. This is an irrevocable reality of the culture of evangelical believers because it is the everyday reality of the biblical world they live in.

Professor Rogers seems to want to recognize this principle of Scripture when he quotes the Westminster Confession, a document at the heart of conservative Christian hermeneutics, their *Magna Carta* of biblical interpretation:

The Supreme Judge, by which all controversies of religion are to be determined, and all decrees of councils, opinions of ancient writers, doctrines of men, and private spirits, are to be examined, and in whose sentence we are to rest, can be no other but the Holy Spirit speaking in the Scripture.[40]

Scripture interpreting Scripture is foundational, constituting everything that gives life and meaning, faith and morals to evangelicals. This significant difference in liberal culture compared to that of evangelicals tempers the entire process of biblical interpretation.

THE "LAW OF CHRIST" AS OUR GUIDE

Coming back to the Old Testament Scriptures, Rogers says in his study of Leviticus that "ritual purity was considered necessary to distinguish the Israelites from their pagan neighbors."[41] His point follows that, unlike the external holiness laws of Moses, "Jesus was concerned with purity of the heart."[42] Here Rogers contrasts the cultural law of Moses with the interior holiness commanded by the Lord Jesus and fulfilled by him.

Rogers explains: "When we see Jesus as the fulfillment of the law (Matt. 5:17), we understand that our challenge is not meticulously to maintain culturally conditioned laws, but rather, with Jesus, to love God and love our neighbor (Matt. 22:36-40)."[43] External purity, or the practice of any cultural holiness, has been replaced with purity of the heart by the inward person.

It must be recognized that it was Jesus himself who warned about the evil that can proceed from the heart:

> Do you not see that whatever goes into the mouth enters the stomach, and goes out into the sewer? But what comes out of the mouth proceeds from the heart, and that is what defiles. For out of the heart come evil intentions, murder, adultery, fornication, theft, false witness, slander. These are what defile a person.
>
> MATTHEW 15:17-19

The inner heart needs to know what is right and wrong—it needs the support and help of the law. Sexual promiscuity and adultery, Jesus says above, come from the inner life. But we only know from scriptural principles that promiscuity and adultery are sin. How do we discern whether what comes out of the heart is morally good or bad except by the law that helps us to know the difference?

While St. Paul brilliantly declared salvation to be all of grace ("For by grace you have saved through faith, and this is not your own doing; it is the gift of God—not the result of works, so that no one may boast," Ephesians 2:8), yet he knew the absolute necessity of law, calling it "the school master" that teaches and guides humankind to receive the free gift of forgiveness offered by grace alone (Galatians 3:24).

As Christians, we all confess our salvation by grace through faith alone. However, we must never forget what our Lord and Savior Jesus Christ has given us in his teachings—like the Sermon on the Mount in the gospels and what St. Paul calls in his letters the "law of Christ"—to guide us in our daily living. Remnants of Moses's "Holiness Code" continue their authority in significant passages in the New Testament.

The central truths of the life, death, and resurrection of our Lord Jesus Christ, and the inward purity of the heart, while central to Christian theology and ethics, do not nullify or diminish the authority of the teachings on sexual morality in other parts of Scripture, like Leviticus, when these Scriptures do not conflict with the gospels and do accord with the central facts of Christ.

COLLISION OF INTERPRETATIONS

Rogers concludes:

> When these texts in Leviticus are taken out of their historical and cultural context and applied to faithful, God-worshipping Christians who are homosexuals, it does violence to them. They are being condemned for failing to conform to an ancient culturally conditioned code that is not applicable to them or their circumstances.[44]

Here we face the collision of his reinterpretation of Scripture with the culture of church scholars who still recognize the repeated parts of the Holiness Code of Moses in the New Testament. The Church Doctrine Committee of the Presbyterian Church in Canada also offered a summary statement on homosexuality and the Bible:

> We do, however, also maintain a number of the laws of Leviticus, mostly notably, perhaps, a certain injunction to love one's neighbor. Many of the regulations that deal with sexual matters, laws dealing with incest, bestiality and adultery, are also still widely accepted. Moreover many are finding new value in the laws there which deal with the poor. In other words, we may neither automatically accept nor reject as authoritative any particular commandment in Leviticus. We must always consider them in their wider canonical context. Does the law in question accord with the key themes in the rest of scripture? Is it contradicted or declared invalid at some other point in scripture? Does it accord with the work and witness of Jesus Christ?
>
> Heterosexuality is considered to be a basic and fundamental part of human nature as God created it. There is no point in the Old Testament at which it can be said that homosexual acts are viewed with any favor at all. The basic understanding of Genesis that humans are created to be heterosexual is accepted by the Jesus of the Gospels, Mt. 19:3–12, Mk. 10:2–12. The regulations of Leviticus 18 and 20 are fully in accord with this key biblical line of understanding. They are part of the trajectory which simply cannot be justifiably removed from the Bible.[45]

Yes, some injunctions of the Holiness Code have been dropped and are no longer in use because the new lawgiver, Jesus Christ, the Messiah, lived out and fulfilled all the Old Testament laws and has set some aside. Messiah Jesus has come and has brought with him, as the Jews believed Messiah would, the new Torah of God, the new Holiness Code of Jesus Christ.

The Lord Jesus Christ gave us many "laws," or guidelines for faith and morality in the gospels, found in the Sermon on the Mount, the parables, and many of his teachings to the crowds. Not only that, but we must remember that the entire remainder of the New Testament was inspired by the Holy Spirit who proceeds from the Father and the Son, meaning the further New Testament "laws" outside the gospels were inspired by the Holy Spirit sent by Jesus Christ. These fill out the new Torah of Messiah Jesus, which includes, as we will see in the next two chapters on the New Testament, teachings on homosexuality.

That new Holiness Code, called in the New Testament "the law of Jesus" (Galatians 6:2) and "the perfect law, the law of liberty" (James 1:25), refines some of the commands and penalties of the Old and sets others aside, but it also affirms many of the teachings that "God spoke to Moses" in Leviticus, including the view of homosexuality.

Acceptance of the Old Testament teachings against homosexuality does not always solve how we are to relate and minister to GLBT people. Tragically, the conservative attack on homosexuals has too often led to the insensitive rejection of hurting people, causing families to be broken or to fall into conflict, instilling hatred toward homosexuals, and even giving rise to physical violence or causing thoughts and acts of suicide by victims of discrimination.

This book stands with gays and lesbians, and everyone else, who will have none of this! We want to love our neighbor. While we affirm Scripture, we want to liberate a persecuted minority and embrace them in our hearts and fellowship. Yet we know God's heart is for us to still "speak the truth in love." I believe we can share the grace and the Torah of the gospels, and still love and accept all those who are fearful and anxious about feelings of same-sex attraction. The key to our relationship with homosexuals is what conservatives have found to be the answers to our own deepest longings—the unmerited grace of Christ, the warm acceptance of God's people, and the wonderful healing of forgiveness.

Turning to the New Testament on homosexuality, we find books written by those living within the fulfillment of Old Testament promises and prophecies as revealed in the life, death, and resurrection of Jesus Christ. And we find that they do directly address homosexuality. What did the New Testament change?

Chapter 4

HOMOSEXUALITY IN THE NEW TESTAMENT

B ecause the New Testament tells of God's answer to all our broken lives and broken laws, we must ask: in the context of grace and forgiveness, what does it say about homosexuality? Does the debate on sexual relations end with the negative references in the Old Testament?

No, the issue of sexuality continues in Scripture. As we have already seen on the positive side, Jesus sanctioned the marriage of a man and a woman, and so the trajectory continues to emerge of the acceptance of monogamous, opposite-gender marriage as the design of God.

Even aside from that, however, homosexuality is directly addressed in the New Testament—so we are not left simply with inferences and implications. In this chapter, we will study three important references to homosexuality in the New Testament, two of which come from the apostle Paul: 1 Corinthians 6:9, 1 Timothy 1:10, and Jude:5–7. In the next chapter, we will examine Paul's Epistle to the Romans 1:18–32.

FIRST CORINTHIANS 6:9–10

There are three expansive and consecutive chapters in the New Testament that focus almost exclusively on sex and marriage—1 Corinthians, chapters 5, 6, and 7—and likewise, three consecutive chapters in the Old Testament on marriage and sexual immorality—Proverbs, chapters 5, 6, and 7.

Many, many references can be found in the Bible that speak to sexuality and marriage, but these two sections are the longest and most comprehensive passages on singleness, sexuality, marriage, and sexual immorality in the entire Bible. And in the middle of St. Paul's chapters on sex and marriage in 1 Corinthians, i.e. in chapter 6:9–10, Paul makes explicit reference to homosexuality.

Paul wrote his first letter to the Christians in Corinth under troubling circumstances. The apostle Paul had founded the Christian congregation in Corinth, the second largest city outside Rome, a port city and merchant trade center with a population of about half a million people. It was not a natural habitat for a faith that emphasized purity! Immorality in Corinth was so rampant that "to corinthicize" had the meaning across the Roman Empire of abandoning moral principles altogether; the word is still listed as meaning "immorality" in archaic English in dictionaries today. On the hills just outside the city of Corinth, female temple prostitutes practiced much of their trade with the sailors who would frequent their city.

Not unexpectedly, after Paul left on further missions, word came back to him of perplexing immorality in the church there. Paul exclaimed to them:

There is sexual immorality among you, and of a kind that is not found even among pagans; for a man is living with his father's wife.

1 Corinthians 5:1

The next chapter, 1 Corinthians 6, refers to Christians taking fellow Christians to court before an unbelieving judge, but a bit later Paul returns to his theme of sexual immorality. Paul lists unrighteous acts which will bring God's judgment, acts which were even done by some in the church, as he prepares the reader for his treatise on singleness and marriage in chapter 7.

In the list of sins written to the immoral Corinthians, the apostle Paul includes references to homosexuality practiced in Corinth:

Do you not know that the unrighteous will not inherit the kingdom of God? Do not be deceived; neither *fornicators [pornoi]*, nor idolaters, nor *adulterers [moikoi]*, nor *effeminate [malakoi]*, nor *homosexuals [arsenokoites]*, nor thieves, nor the covetous, nor drunkards, nor revilers, nor swindlers, will inherit the kingdom of God.

1 Corinthians 6:9–10, NASB; *ITALICS MINE*

The word "fornication," *pornoi* in Greek, gives us the word *pornography*. In Greek, it referred to premarital sex by one or both partners, as found among heterosexuals.[46] Paul's next word for sexual immorality is "adultery," *moikoi* in Greek, which has the exclusive sense of sexual relations committed outside of heterosexual marriage.[47]

We must remember that the Bible's condemnation of fornication and adultery among heterosexuals is the focus here, much as we find in Proverbs 5, 6, and 7 in the warnings given by a father to his son in lengthy lyrical teachings without any references to homosexuality. The Bible speaks very sparingly of same-gender sexual relations, possibly because it was found infrequently in Bible history, unlike the constant, urgent warnings against fornication and adultery. We can never single out homosexuality in the Bible without the more devastating and universal warnings found often in Scripture against fornication and adultery.

Having mentioned two heterosexual sins, Paul progresses to two other sexual sins which some scholars believe refer to homosexual sins. These words are "effeminate," *malakoi* in Greek, and "homosexuals," *arsenokoite* in Greek. The Greek word *malakois* appears in both Matthew 11:8 and Luke 7:25, where Jesus speaks of those in king's palaces dressed in "soft" or "delicate" *(malakois)* clothing in contrast with the rough and outspoken John the Baptist, who was dressed in coarse camel's hair.

The Jerusalem Bible translates this word *malakoi* as "catamite," meaning a "sodomite's minion," that is, the passive, "soft," "delicate," or "effeminate" male partner in homosexual acts.[48]

When we combine this word *malakoi* with the next word in this list, *arsenokoite,* often translated "male homosexual" but translated in the Revised Standard Version and New Revised Standard Version Bibles as "sodomite," we find in these two words both the active and passive partners in homosexual unions. This is the same meaning clarified in a footnote on this passage in the English Standard Version of the Bible: "The two Greek terms translated by this phrase refer to the passive and active partners in consensual homosexual acts."[49]

We will further examine Paul's use of *arsenokoite* in a moment, but in summary, in 1 Corinthians 6:9 Paul reiterates Moses's words in Leviticus

18 and 20 that the believer's conduct should be very different from that of the surrounding nonbelievers and that the Christians, like the ancient Israelites, should hold to a different standard of sexual behavior than that of other nations. And Paul confirms the prohibition against homosexuality in Leviticus in full agreement.

FIRST TIMOTHY 1:9

The word *arsenokoite* also occurs in Paul's first pastoral letter to his son in the faith, Timothy:

> Now we know that the law is good, if one uses it legitimately. This means understanding that the law is laid down not for the innocent but for the lawless and disobedient, for the godless and sinful, for the unholy and profane, for those who kill their father or mother, for murderers, fornicators, sodomites *[arsenokoitais]* and slave traders, liars, perjurers and whatever else is contrary to the sound teaching.
>
> 1 TIMOTHY 1:8–10

This Greek word is a compound word coined by Paul, appearing here and in 1 Corinthians 6:9 for the first time in any Greek literature, and contains the root words *arsen* (male) and *koites* (bed). Both pro-gay scholars and conservative scholars agree that Paul refers in this term to sexual sin, but they disagree on what kind of sin is implied.

Jack Rogers dismisses this compound word very quickly, in less than two pages, as having little reference to homosexuality, especially as we know GLBT people today, by quoting several liberal scholars who show the difficulty of "linguistic technicality" in discerning the meaning of this word Paul uses. The scholars he cites are Brian Blount, who says the meaning of these words is "not at all clear"; Martti Nissinen, who says Paul's compound word "is difficult to understand"; Dale Martin, who looks at the Greek writings after Paul that use this compound word and demonstrate a different meaning than consenting homosexual men; Victor Furnish, who cites the order of sins in Paul's sin list and suggests that "sodomites" is not a biblical word, probably meaning "sexual exploiters of some sort," and is not a reference to mutually agreed-upon adult homosexuality; and Marion Soards, who believes there is no direct meaning "regarding homosexuality from this material."[50] These scholarly writings were published between 1994 and 1998.

JOHN BOSWELL

An even earlier analysis of homosexuality, written in 1980 yet still a powerful pro-gay apologetic, comes from gay historian John Boswell in his long and substantive book, *Christianity, Social Tolerance and Homosexuality*, in which Boswell carefully examines this Pauline word. Like the scholars Rogers quotes on this word, Boswell argues that the word used by Paul in 1 Corinthians 6:9 and 1 Timothy 1:9 has no reference to consenting homosexual men, but only to prostitution or immoral behavior overall. Boswell writes:

> *Arsenokoite,* then, means "male sex agents, i.e. active male prostitutes, who were common throughout the Hellenistic world in the time of Paul...male prostitutes capable of the active role with either men or women.[51]

If Boswell is correct, then Paul's term *arsenokoites* has no relevance to contemporary mutually consenting adult men.

But is the case really so cut-and-dried? The two root words for this constructed term should be examined carefully. We quote from an authoritative book by ex-gay minister Joe Dallas in *The Gay Gospel?* Dallas writes:

> *Arsenos* refers to a male (or males—*arsenes)* with an emphasis on their gender. *Koite* appears only twice in the New Testament, and means bed or couch in a sexual connotation:

> Let us walk honestly...not in chambering (*koite*).

> ROMANS 13:13 KJV

Marriage is honorable…and the bed (*koite*) undefiled

Hebrews 13:4

The first striking point about Paul's use of these two words when creating the term *arsenokoite* is that there is nothing in the words male or bed implying trade, buying, or selling, making Boswell's guess that the term referred to prostitution, an unlikely one. These two words, as Paul combined them, put male and bed together in a sexual sense, with no hint of prostitution involved.[52]

Boswell and scholar Dale Martin (cited by Rogers) do find in later Christian and secular uses of the word *arsenokoite* something more general, meaning "some kind of economic exploitation, probably by sexual means: rape or sex by economic coercion, prostitution…"[53]

Joe Dallas says that these scholars can say this, "but in so doing, even if their intent was clear, it would be a technical misuse of the word."[54] Dallas continues to make a strong point:

Arsenokoite (*males* combined with *bed* or *couch*) is as Timothy Dailey points out, the Greek counterpart to the Hebrew phrase *mishkab zakur. Mishkab* is Hebrew for *bed* or *couch* with a sexual connotation; *zakur* in Hebrew means male or males. The phrase *mishkab zakur* is found in Leviticus 18:22 and 20:13, where sex between men is expressly forbidden.[55]

The connection with Leviticus is completed when we see that the Septuagint, the Greek translation of the Old Testament (Greek being the common language of the Roman Empire from the time of Alexander the Great, who conquered the region three hundred years earlier) was the frequent source for reading the Old Testament in Paul's era.

Dallas observes that the Septuagint uses the terms *arsenos* and *koite* side by side when translating prohibitions against homosexuality in the original Hebrew in those same passages in Leviticus:

"You shall not lie with a male as with a woman; it is an abomination."

LEVITICUS 18:22, NRSV

Meta *arsenos* ou koimethese *koite* gyniakos
"If a man lies with a male as with a woman, both of them have committed an abomination."

LEVITICUS. 20:13

Hos an koimethe meta *arsenos koite* gynaikos

Here are the two words *arsenos* and *koite,* making Paul's compound word when taken together, appearing side by side in the Septuagint. In conclusion, Dallas gives a summary of what is the most apparent and clear sense of *arsenokoite* when Paul uses it in 1 Corinthians 6:9 and 1 Timothy 1:10:

When Paul coined the word *arsenokoite,* he took it directly from the Greek translation of Leviticus's prohibitions against homosexual behavior. His intent couldn't be clearer. Though *arsenokoite* is unique to Paul, it refers specifically and unambiguously to sex between men.[56]

The Presbyterian Church in Canada's Church Doctrine Committee judiciously decided on the meaning of these words in 1 Corinthians 6:9 to be as follows, with a decision with which Dallas appears in full agreement:

Here it is declared that "malakoi" (literally, the "soft") and "arsenokoite," among others, will not inherit the Kingdom of God. The latter word also appears in a second sin list in 1 Timothy 1:8–10. It is a relatively rare word (the Pauline usage is its earliest appearance) and a valiant attempt has been made by various scholars to deny that it necessarily refers to homosexuals at all. While detailed arguments cannot be presented here it must be noted that the unusual word is very probably a literal translation of the rabbinic term for male homosexual activity "mishkav zakur", or "lying with a male." The Greek word is a compound one, made of the words for "male" and "bed". The latter is used euphemistically in a way that should not be unfamiliar to us. The two words are found in the Septuagint version of the laws of Leviticus considered earlier.[57]

Professor Jack Rogers makes his bold conclusion: "Once again, careful attention to the linguistic, historical and cultural context has led to a richer and more nuanced understanding of the plain text."[58]

But after examining the underlying language and context, one wonders if Rogers' conviction is the result of careful, deliberate biblical interpretation, or only a matter of inventing the meaning of the text, knowing in advance and deliberately aiming for where he already wants to end up!

JUDE 5–7

Jude was the brother of James, the leader of the Jerusalem church following the resurrection of the Lord Jesus Christ. He wrote only this brief letter in the New Testament. Jude wrote this epistle, probably after the fall of Jerusalem and the death of Peter, quoting Peter's second letter in verses 17 and 18.[59]

Jude was reacting to false teaching and immoral practices that had crept into the church, which some scholars believe represented an early form of Gnosticism.[60] In his blistering attack, reminiscent of Jesus's condemnation of the Pharisees in Matthew 23, Jude excoriates these false teachers. He gives illustrations of God's judgment against characters in the Old Testament like Cain, Balaam, Korah, and the children of Israel in the desert. Jude also makes references to two nonbiblical books, Enoch and the Assumption of Moses.

Thomas E. Schmidt, in his book *Straight and Narrow: Compassion and Clarity in the Homosexual Debate,* points out that Jude makes reference to homosexuality in this New Testament epistle.[61] Jude writes to his readers about the judgment God brought upon Sodom and Gomorrah:

> And the angels who did not keep their own position, but left their proper dwelling, he has kept in eternal chains in deepest darkness for the judgment of the great Day. Likewise, Sodom and Gomorrah and the surrounding cities, which, in the same manner as they, indulged in sexual immorality and pursued unnatural lust [Greek literally, "went after other flesh"] serve as an example by undergoing a punishment of eternal fire.
>
> JUDE 6–7

Jude gives this illustration from the Old Testament of God's punishment of wrongdoers to warn those who had disrupted the early Christian church. The words clearly refer to the cities of Sodom and Gomorrah, which suffered "eternal fire" because of "sexual immorality." Recall from chapter 3 that the sexual sin of the men of Sodom was seen in their wanting to "know," i.e. have sexual intercourse with, other males ("angels").

There is a double meaning in Jude between "angels" and humankind. The reference in Jude 6, "And the angels who did not keep their own position, but left their proper dwelling," goes back to Genesis 6:1–4, where it is said that the "sons of God," usually interpreted as "angels," came down from their proper habitation in heaven to take wives on earth of the "daughters of men."

This account represents a glimpse of the terrible universal evil at the time of Noah. The act of the fallen angels having "unnatural lust," or literally in the Greek, "going after other flesh," to take wives of human females is parallel to the sins of the men of Sodom in going after the unnatural flesh of the male angels sheltered in Lot's house. Schmidt observes: "The first Christians undoubtedly connected the sin of Sodom to the sin of same-sex relations."[62]

Professor Rogers acknowledges that Jude uses the terms "sexual immorality" and "unnatural lust" to refer to the sins of the males of

Sodom, but he adds, "For Schmidt, or anyone else, to make the leap that this text somehow condemns present-day Christians who are homosexual strikes me as bizarre."[63] The connection may appear unfair and bizarre to Rogers, but these are the words and references in the text.

To clarify whether these references to homosexuality in the New Testament passages of 1 Corinthians, 1 Timothy, and Jude speak of gays and lesbians as we know them in the world today, we will now turn to Paul's most theological and full expression of the gospel in his Epistle to the Romans.

Chapter 5

GAYS, LESBIANS, AND ST. PAUL

S
ome scholars cite St. Paul's words in Romans 1:18–32 as the single most important Scripture on the topic of homosexuality.[64] While conservatives have long held this passage as an important proof text against the morality of homosexual lifestyles, revisionists argue quite a different conclusion. Many ideas have been connected to the passage in Romans 1:18–32, and Professor Rogers cites many different authorities as he addresses it. As before, though, we must ask whether their conclusions are fair to the words of the text. We will proceed through the passage verse by verse, referring to commentaries as we go.

The reader must pay close attention to determine whether the revisionists are correct in dismissing Romans 1:18-32 as only condemning idolatry or as having only a regional meaning to Paul and those around him in the Judaic/Hellenistic culture of their own time. They deny that Romans 1 has any "creation pattern" for sexual relationships—not for people generally, and especially not for gays and lesbians. If they are correct in their interpretation, then revisionists like Rogers are right to reject this passage as having any reference to the faithful, believing gays and lesbians we find in the church today. But does their interpretation really hold up?

Paul launches his theological epistle to the Christians in Rome with this opening thesis:

> For I am not ashamed of the gospel; it is the power of God for salvation to everyone who has faith, to the Jew first and also the Greek. For in it the righteousness of God is revealed through

faith for faith; as it is written, "The one who is righteous will live by faith."

Romans 1:16–17, citing Habakkuk 2:4

Paul's main idea in writing this letter to the Christians in Rome was to express the essential meaning of the life, death, and resurrection of Jesus Christ. This is the gospel of a tiny, humble minority of believers amidst the immense grandeur of paganism all around them. Despite all this, Paul is not ashamed of his gospel.

In this opening section, Paul speaks of the righteousness that comes by faith, a topic he will greatly expand upon throughout the epistle from the insight God revealed to him. For Paul, verses 16–17 are the essence of the gospel. Rogers agrees that in 1:16–17, Paul states the thesis of his letter.[65] From that thesis, we proceed into the heart of our topic as Paul begins to demonstrate the nature of sin and estrangement from God.

Paramount to understanding this whole section of Scripture, we must note the parallel structure in this chapter between what is "natural" and what is "unnatural." First, Paul begins with the immense contrast between God (our "natural" relationship is to have faith in this Creator God) and creaturely things (the "unnatural" relationship of making idols from creation).

Here God the Creator stands on one side:

For what can be known about God is plain to them, because God has shown it to them. Ever since the creation of the world his eternal power and divine nature, invisible though they are, have been understood and seen through the things he has made. So they are without excuse.

Romans 1:18–20

The Creator is known by the things he has made. Most Bibles reference Psalm 19:1–6 as a companion Old Testament Scripture to this passage in Romans 1:20: "The heavens are telling the glory of God; and the firmament proclaims his handiwork" (Psalm 19:1). Calvin called creation "the theatre of God's glory."[66] Many historical theological works begin with our knowledge of God from the natural world.

St. Paul states this to be our created, wholesome, and "natural" state: to believe in the Creator's "eternal power and divine nature...through the things he has made." He says all people are "without excuse" for not having this "natural" faith in God.

Now, on the other side, stands the idolatry of creation. Paul writes of an enormous "unnatural" act of many people toward their Creator, by turning away from God to manufacture and worship creaturely idols:

> For though they knew God, they did not honor him as God or give thanks to him, but they became futile in their thinking, and their senseless minds were darkened. Claiming to be wise, they became fools; and they exchanged the glory of the immortal God for images resembling a mortal human being or birds or four-footed animals or reptiles.
>
> Therefore God gave them up to the lusts of their hearts to impurity, to the degrading of their bodies among themselves, because they exchanged the truth about God for a lie and worshipped and served the creature rather than the Creator, who is blessed forever! Amen.
>
> ROMANS 1:21–25

Here we find Paul's counterpoint between the created, "natural" worship of the Creator and the impure and "unnatural" making and worshiping of idols.

Rogers wants to stop here and say that this is the only main point Paul is making in this first chapter of Romans. He writes: "In Romans 1:18–32, Paul is writing about idolatry, that is worshipping, giving our ultimate allegiance, to anything in the creation instead of God, the Creator."[67]

However, it is clear that this is not the "only main point" Paul is making in Romans 1. Paul continues his parallelism from faith in the Creator (a natural act) and the worship of idols (humankind's unnatural act) to a second series of natural and unnatural realities in a second disorder of creation, this time in reference to sexuality.

In verses 26–27 below, Paul makes the very important point for his Christian readers in Rome that just as unnatural idol worship is contrary to the natural function of man according to the way we were made, immoral man's unnatural sexual relations must be clearly stated and resisted:

> For this reason God gave them up to dishonorable passions. For their women exchanged *natural relations* for those that are *contrary to nature*, and the men likewise gave up *natural relations* with women and were consumed with passion for one another, men committing shameless acts with men and receiving in themselves the due penalty for their error.
>
> ROMANS 1:26–27, ESV; *ITALICS MINE*

In this passage, unnatural sexuality is every bit as important a sign of rebellion against the Creator as unnatural idolatry. While Professor Rogers insists Romans 1 is "primarily about idolatry,"[68] it is just as much about the continuing pattern of moral disintegration within the whole pattern of rebellion against the Creator that Paul goes on to expose in detail.

Continuing his theme of natural and unnatural acts, Paul now writes about the specific disorder in sexual relationships. *The ESV Study Bible* comments on this new theme on homosexuality in Romans 1:26–27:

> Just as idolatry is unnatural (contrary to what God intended when he made human beings), so too homosexuality is "contrary to nature" in that it does not represent what God intended when he made men and women with physical bodies that have a "natural" way of interacting with each other. Paul follows the Old Testament and Jewish tradition in seeing all homosexual relationships as sinful. The creation account in Genesis 1–2 reveals the divine paradigm for human beings, indicating that God's will is for men and women to be joined in marriage.[69]

Another Bible commentator, Dr. Harold Lindsell, writing in the *NRSV Harper Study Bible,* notes that this passage traces the path of the fall of the human race:

> The human race retrogressed after the fall. People turned from serving one God to serving idols and from purity to adultery, fornication, and perverse sin against nature itself. At last "God gave them up...to things that should not be done."[70]

There is a downward collapse from what humankind was first created to be into human rejection of their natural relationship to their Creator, into unnatural idolatry, and then a further slide down into unnatural sexual relations with one another.

Paul uses the term "God gave them up" three times in Romans 1 to emphasize God's rejection of humankind because of their progressive degeneration into sin:

> "Therefore *God gave them up* in the lusts of their hearts to impurity" (v. 24).
> "For this reason *God gave them up* to degrading passions" (v. 26).
> "*God gave them up* to a debased mind" (v. 28).

Dr. Lindsell makes this observation of man's retrogressive fall:

> Paul uses this phrase (God gave them up) three times: (1) he gave them up to using sexual relations in a wrong fashion, i.e., fornication and adultery; (2) he gave them up to using sexual relations in a perverse way, i.e., homosexual conduct; and (3) he gave them up to a debased mind, so that they called evil good and defended those who did the things described in vv. 24–32.[71]

Romans 1:28–32, which ends the first chapter, lists twenty-two other things that immoral man does, including things as common as gossip and haughty behavior and extending to the most serious offenses of murder, hatred of God, and committing ruthless acts.

It should be noted that Paul emphasizes the term "exchanged" in connection with humankind's rejection of what is natural in exchange for what is unnatural:

"They *exchanged* the glory of the immortal God for images" (v. 22).
"They *exchanged* the truth of God for a lie" (v. 25).
"Their women *exchanged* natural sexual relations for unnatural" (v. 26).

Professor Rogers raises a number of problems with the traditional, conservative interpretation of Romans 1:18–32, some of which we will deal with here: (1) the creation pattern or cultural norms, (2) gender roles, (3) passionate or controlled sex, (4) irrelevant idolatry, and a fifth item raised by John Boswell, (5) heterosexual, not homosexual, sin.

CREATION THEME OR MERELY ANCIENT CULTURE?

Can we understand what Paul meant by the words "natural" and "unnatural" in Romans 1:26–27? In these two verses, Paul uses the Greek words *physis* (nature) and *para physin* (contrary to nature). *Physis* can mean slightly different things in different contexts in the New Testament. In Galatians 4:8 it means *native condition* or *birth*; in Galatians 2:15 it again means *birth*; in Romans 2:14 it means *nature* or *native instinct*; and in Ephesians 2:3 it means *native species* or *kind*.[72]

We see here in Romans 1:26 and 27 that "natural," *physis,* is closest in the text to the meaning in Romans 2:14 in the next chapter, where it is translated "nature," and it must be understood in the context in which it is used and not based on another unrelated use of the word. Professor Rogers tries to employ Romans 11:13–24 for interpreting *physis* and then attempts to apply it to our passage in Romans 1:26–27. He points out that through unbelief (v. 23) the "natural" branches of Israel were broken off from the true olive tree of God, and the "unnatural" branches of the "wild olive tree," representing the "wild" alien race of the now-believing

Gentiles, were grafted in. Rogers tries to make the point that "for Paul 'unnatural' is a synonym for 'unconventional.'"[73] Rogers' sees God's pruning as "unconventional," not as "something contrary to nature" or "against nature" as the words are usually interpreted in the passage in Romans 1. Thus *para physin* is something acting only in a "surprising and out of the ordinary way."[74]

Rogers concludes, "In speaking about what is 'natural,' Paul is merely accepting the conventional view of people and how they ought to behave in first-century Hellenistic-Jewish culture."[75]

In saying in reference to the homosexuals in Romans 1:26–27 that "unnatural" only means "something surprisingly out of the ordinary,"[76] Rogers asserts that homosexuality should not be seen as a violation of "creation," i.e. the way God made the universe, humankind, and nature; rather, Paul's wording indicates only an innocent, "unconventional" sexual relationship for same-sex partners, only "surprisingly" different, with relevance only to Paul and the Greek-Jewish culture of his day.

The problem with Rogers' interpretation is that (a) the reference to the natural and unnatural olive branches in Romans 11:13–24 clearly points to God's engrafting Gentiles who are not just "different" but are more accurately "unnatural," as aliens to the true Israel, in this sense, and that he can do so without any violation of his own purity or justice; and (b) we must take the meaning for the term "unnatural relations" in Romans 1 only from the context in which it is used *in that passage.*

We must remember that in Romans 1:18–32 Paul clearly structures the passage using parallelism: first showing the creation theme of natural belief in God contrasted with the unnatural turn to idolatry and then showing natural and unnatural sexual relationships with the same contrast. For Paul, the parallelism of natural and unnatural in both idolatry and homosexuality is based on the way God created the universe. Thus, both the acts of idolatry and homosexuality violate God's revealed creation pattern for humankind.

In other words, Paul does not merely look at homosexuality through an obsolete cultural lens—as something merely "unconventional" and "out of the ordinary." Rather, the "unnatural relations" of the homosexuals, illuminated by Paul in the context of God's natural plan for the universe, demonstrate that humankind's fall into idolatry and unnatural living are not just culturally limited to Paul's era, but stand as violations of God's creation plan for all times, in all places.

Gender Roles

Rogers makes many reference to Martti Nissinen's book *Homoeroticism in the Biblical World: A Historical Perspective,* especially Nissinen's observations on gender roles for men and women in Paul's day. Nissinen says that sexual physiology is not as important as gender role for Paul. "Paul's understanding of the naturalness of men's and women's gender role is not a matter of genital formation and their functional purpose, which today is considered by many the main criterion for the natural and unnatural," Nissinen writes.[77]

Rogers adds to this: "Rather, in the culture that Paul is addressing, a man and a woman each had a designated place and role in society, which could not be exchanged."[78] Rogers backs this up with Paul's appeal for men to have short hair and women to have long hair, which is based on their distinct gender roles that cannot be violated. "Does not nature itself teach you this," Paul writes to his readers in 1 Corinthians 11:14, urging them to follow their gender roles, which if violated, Rogers says, "would be a matter of shame before God."[79] Rogers' point here is that the offense of these women is crossing their gender role rather than same-sex impropriety.

Nissinen and Rogers try to assert that "for Paul, transgression of gender role boundaries causes 'impurity,' a violation of the Jewish purity code."[80] Rogers explains that the text doesn't say that women acted improperly with other women, but that the women exchanged natural relations, meaning they "could have been condemned for taking the dominant position in heterosexual intercourse, or for engaging in non-productive sexual acts with male partners. The issue is gender dominance and gender roles in a culture where women were to be passive and not active in sexual matters."[81]

This statement is perplexing, not just because there is no basis in all of Scripture for speaking of "a dominant sexual position" or women's "nonproductive sexual acts," or even being "passive and not active in sexual matters," but also because the "women who exchanged natural relations" in Romans 1:26 didn't just transgress gender roles but were placed in the same parallel context as the men who "likewise gave up natural relations with women and were consumed with passion for one another" (Romans 1:27).

It must be added that women crossed over, or even violated with impunity, gender roles in the Bible—like Deborah in the Old Testament, who not only served as Israel's highest authority as judge in an observant patriarchal culture, but also as their military general in battle; Miriam, Moses's sister, who served as a prophet at the side of Moses; Anna, a prophetess, who was stationed in the Jerusalem temple when the infant Jesus was brought in for his rites; Mary Magdalene, who was the first to be entrusted to take the gospel message of the risen Lord back to the upper room to tell the disciples; the evangelist Philip's four unmarried daughters, who all served God by prophesying. Our Lord Jesus Christ himself took the role of a servant (possibly, could we say, even a female role?) in washing the feet of his disciples. Some of these examples of women crossing gender roles have formed the theological basis for many Protestant churches in North America ordaining women as elders and ministers. Gender roles were somewhat fluid in even this male-dominated Old and New Testament culture.

Notwithstanding, Romans 1:27 doesn't speak of the violation of gender roles and the place of males and females in society, but of the deliberate choosing of "unnatural relations" of men with other men, and in that same context, of women with other women. Much more is at stake than what Rogers and Nissinen suggest.

PASSIONATE OR CONTROLLED SEX

Even more extraordinary is Rogers' attempt to redefine the "dishonorable passion" of the women and the "shameless acts" of the men in Romans 1:26–27 as only the violation of the prevailing Stoic ideal of everything in moderation. In Paul's culture, Rogers writes, "the goal was to make correct 'use' of all things. The 'natural use' of sex was to be very controlled, avoiding passion."[82] Rogers observes that verses 26 and 27 are not about "wrongly oriented desires, but inordinate desires—going to excess, losing control."[83]

Paul's sermon to the Athenians at Mars Hill shows he is familiar with Greek poetry and Greek philosophy, probably knowing the Stoic dictum of "moderation in everything," but much more importantly, Paul knows the divine approval of the breathless passion of young lovers in the Song of Songs in the Old Testament and Jacob's passionate love for Rachel, whom he sacrificed years of hard labor to win. It's difficult to think of any sexual relations between men and women without powerful passion and emotional excitement! For Rogers to talk about "controlled" sex and "avoiding passion" sounds like he is saying the Bible holds only the lost memories of romance, like some may feel after years of disillusioned living—a cynicism which the Bible nowhere upholds as the model for sexual relations. The problem in Romans 1:26–27 is not with "inordinate" sexual passion; rather, it is all about wrongly directed sexual desire leading to unnatural sexual relations.

It should be mentioned here that sometimes gays and lesbians feel this passage in Romans 1:26–27 doesn't apply to them because they feel they do not burn with "dishonorable passion," nor do they do "shameless acts" with multiple partners. It may be said that like many heterosexuals, some gays and lesbians have long-term partners, and where available, others have successful marriages. They just don't do "shameless" indiscriminate sex with many people, they say, nor are they "consumed with passion" for their special partner whom they sensitively care for and love. It appears that this is the image that Professor Rogers has of gays and lesbians today who, he feels, are not represented in the Bible's references to homosexuality.

Ex-gay minister Joe Dallas answers this justification of the pro-gay advocate:

Nothing in (Paul's) phrasing or choice of words states, or even implies, that they were doing it with many people of the same sex, or that they were doing it frequently or randomly. In other words, Paul condemns the thing itself, without qualifying the condemnation to apply only to homosexuality practiced "irresponsibly" or with many partners. Like adultery and fornication, it's no less a sin if it's committed once in a life time with one partner; no more a sin if it's committed daily with several partners. The condemnation here is of the thing itself, not the way it is practiced.[84]

IRRELEVANT IDOLATRY

Consider next the pro-gay apologist who says that Romans 1:18–32 applies just to those who practice idolatry, since they feel this is Paul's only point here, and that it has nothing to do with God-fearing, committed Christian homosexuals. Such advocates feel Paul's condemnation of idolatry doesn't apply to loving, faithful same-sex couples who live in committed relationships. Professor Jack Rogers makes this same point again and again in his book:

> Those who are opposed to equal rights for Christian gay and lesbian people make several serious errors in interpreting Romans 1: (1) they lose sight of the fact that this passage is primarily about idolatry...(4) they apply Paul's condemnation of immoral sexual activity to faithful gay and lesbian Christians who are not idolaters, who love God, and who seek to live in thankful obedience to God.[85]

In Romans 1, Paul develops the reality of idolatry first and most fully. "The pro-gay theorist," Dallas observes, "seizes on this concept to prove that Paul's condemnation of homosexuality does not apply to him."[86] Christian homosexuals today do not see themselves in Romans 1 because they do not manufacture or worship idols. However, we find this helpful quote from Thomas Schmidt:

> Paul is not suggesting that a person worships an idol and decides

therefore to engage in same-sex relations. Rather, he is suggesting that the general rebellion created the environment for the specific rebellion. A person need not bow before a golden calf to participate in the general human denial of God or to express that denial through specific behaviors.[87]

If this passage doesn't apply to homosexuals because today they do not worship idols, can the idolatry interpretation be applied to all the other sins in the catalog of transgressions Paul lists in Romans 1:29–32? Are murder and violent abuse only sins if they are practiced by idolaters, but not if they are practiced by loving, committed people? Dallas answers this:

> This, of course, is ridiculous. Like homosexuality, these sins are not born just out of idol worship; they are symptomatic of a fallen state. If we are to say homosexuality is legitimate so long as it is not a result of idol worship, then we have to say these other sins are legitimate as well…so long as they too are not practiced as the result of idolatry.[88]

HETEROSEXUAL, NOT HOMOSEXUAL SIN

A very popular interpretation of the reference to homosexuals in Romans 1, with many later gay and lesbian followers, came early in the gay movement in a book published in 1980 by the popular linguist and classical historian John Boswell. The idea he presents for understanding the words "exchange natural relations for those that are contrary to nature" (v. 26–27) is that these people were not homosexuals at all, but heterosexuals who violated their own orientation to have sex with the same gender. Boswell writes:

> The persons that Paul condemns are manifestly not homosexual: what he derogates are homosexual acts committed by apparently heterosexual persons. The whole point of Romans 1, in fact, is to stigmatize persons who have rejected their calling, gotten off the true path they were once on.[89]

Dallas cites another quote on this from Scanzoni and Mollenkott:

What Paul seems to be emphasizing here is that persons who are heterosexual by nature have not only exchanged the true God for a false one but have also exchanged their ability to relate to the opposite sex by indulging in homosexual behavior that is not natural *to them.*[90]

What these men are saying is that the sins in Romans 1 rest with heterosexuals who turn away from their own orientation and do something completely unnatural for them by having sexual relations outside their own proper field of relationships with other men. This has nothing to do, Boswell says, with true homosexuals for whom it is a natural thing to have same-sex relations. Dallas observes: "Homosexuality, they contend, if committed by true homosexuals, is, therefore, not a sin and is not referenced here."[91]

The response to Boswell's interpretation comes from studying the words that Paul uses for males, *arsenes,* and females, *theleias.* These words emphasize the physiology of men and women and underscore their gender. Dallas presents this analysis:

Here Paul is very pointedly saying that the homosexual behavior committed by these people was unnatural to them as males and females (*arsenes* and *theleias*), he is not considering any such thing as sexual orientation. He is saying, in other words, that homosexuality is biologically unnatural—not just unnatural to heterosexuals, but unnatural to *anyone.*[92]

Also, the fact that the men in Romans 1 "were consumed with passion for one another" (v. 27) suggests they were not casually exploring other sexual options but had a very strong, inner orientation for same-sex relations.

The last point against Boswell's interpretation is that if you condemn homosexual actions done by men to whom they don't come naturally and allow them for people who have a natural inclination for them, what about all the other sins listed at the end of Romans 1? Do we allow people to commit strife, deceit, and murder if it comes naturally to them? Are these only deemed to be sins if they are committed by people who don't have a natural inclination for them? This double standard could never be accepted and would be a moral absurdity. It must be concluded that the men and women of Romans 1 were homosexuals who "exchanged natural relations for those that are contrary to nature" (v. 26–27).

WHY ALL THIS?

Why have we taken so long to examine the references to homosexuality when there are only eight passages in all of Scripture focusing on the topic? Why all this attention? For that matter, why is this whole issue such a major one in the church today, affecting nearly all of us in some way or other?

It ultimately comes down to the fact that at the heart of it all, for Christians at least, stands the *authority of Scripture!* While the Old and New Testament references to homosexuality may all lead away from the moral acceptance of same-sex sexual relations, Professor Jack Rogers doggedly persists with the point that so-called homosexuality in the Bible has nothing to do with "contemporary Christian people who are homosexual."[93] Rogers gives a telling quote from Professor Jeffrey Siker of Loyola Marymount University:

> We know of gay and lesbian Christians who truly worship and serve the one true God and yet still affirm in positive ways their identity as gay and lesbian people. Paul apparently knew of no homosexual Christians. We do.[94]

This may not be entirely true, because we do not know if Paul knew of believing homosexuals in the church. In fact, we do see in 1 Corinthians 6:11 that Paul writes, following his passage against homosexuality, "And such were some of you." In other words, he may have known homosexuals in the Corinthian church he founded.

Today, many evangelicals know believing gays and lesbians. And they find many to be sincere, committed people. Yet like the apostle Paul, conservative, believing Christians still, despite friendly contact with believing same-sex persons, continue to accept the prohibition of homosexuality found in both the Old and New Testaments. For them, this is not a matter of personal preference, unloving legalism, or opinion. It is about the authority of Scripture.

CTV National News in Canada broadcast a story on the tenth anniversary of the first gay couple and lesbian couples to be married in a joint service here in 2000. The story told a wonderful tale of the faith, commitment, and love between two people again standing at the front of the Metropolitan Community Church in Toronto to renew their vows. The commitment and solemnity of the occasion could be felt by everyone watching, including many evangelicals. The same affection and warmth can be felt by many conservative Christians in the United States and Canada who view the marriages of popular television stars and loved celebrities who form same-gender unions.

What's wrong with Moses and Paul? What's wrong with Christians in our own time who appreciate the happiness of two people and yet remain determined to hold their lifestyle to be against God's plan for sexuality? Why can't believers in the Bible see that today's gays and lesbians are "contemporary Christians," completely unlike those we find in the Bible such as the violent and abusive men of Sodom? What's unnatural about a couple who feel completely at home and natural with who they are and have "pride" in how normal they feel in their sexual relationships with each other?

The reason for this resistance from believing Christians, in essence, comes down to the very difficult task of rightly interpreting the Holy Bible within a Bible-believing culture, and as we will see in the next chapter, holding to the true definition and nature of marriage and the natural law of sexual relationships.

Many evangelicals love people as widely and deeply as revisionists appear to do, but they are guided by the proper, accurate, and historic interpretation of Scripture for our own time. That's why the interpretation of Scripture remains paramount for the church and will always determine the actions, beliefs, and views of the behavior of others for the believing Christian community. To uplift the authority of Scripture as it speaks to gays and lesbians is not an antihomosexual or homophobic thing to do. The attempt has been made to speak the truth in love. It does no one any good to misrepresent the Word of God, and certainly neither the homosexual nor the wider population wants the Christian church to compromise their stand for the sake of relating to popular culture or for popular approval. Faithfulness to God and Scripture must be found and proclaimed in order to build real bridges of reconciliation.

Nevertheless, in this debate it must also be admitted that unless you are a Christian who confesses *Sola Scriptura,* Scripture doesn't answer everything. There are many more dimensions to the gay and lesbian debate than what is decided by Scripture. The evangelical position is tenable even outside of the Bible's direct teachings, and as such, there must be a broader intellectual appeal to gays than from the Bible alone, which may not be viewed as any kind of authority for them and for many other people today.

In the next chapter, we will turn to another dimension of this study found in the philosophical arguments for the definition of the nature of marriage. This rational study of marriage can help guide our thinking about same-sex relationships apart from any views derived from religion or morality.

Theology and rational philosophy sometimes meet in surprising places. Let us now explore the connection between revealed truths and the rational man.

Chapter 6

THE DEFINITION OF MARRIAGE AND THE ROLE OF CIVIL RIGHTS

F ew Protestant scholars appeal to the philosophical arguments for the existence of God from natural theology, nor do they consider the nature and definition of marriage from the rational, philosophical study of the natural order of marriage. Yet these principles should not be ignored in our examination of any issue. However persuasive the arguments from Scripture are for Christians and the church, there can also be rational analysis purely from philosophy, without any reference to Scripture and revealed truth from God. In other words, we can discover "natural law" strictly from a logical analysis of the natural world.

In my earlier book, an apologetic called *Confident Faith in a World that Wants to Believe,* I established the existence of the Creator from the cause and effect of the natural world going back to God as the First Cause.[95] Natural theology, or as it is sometimes called, "common revelation," can become a powerful force in the debate with unbelievers who don't accept the authority of biblical revelation.

St. Paul asserts that the nature of the created world reveals to everyone their Creator. This natural belief in the Creator (i.e. "natural theology") doesn't come from popular prejudice or the simple, unthinking mythologies of ancient civilizations, nor is natural theology *ultra virus* to Scripture. It comes from the way God made the universe and the natural function of humankind to know this!

In his theology, St. Paul appeals to the natural world, which everyone can discover directly for themselves. Beyond Scripture, the natural world that all can touch, see, and experience constitutes the cosmic backdrop for Paul's theology in Romans 1 and elsewhere. The sermon he proclaimed in Athens to the intellectuals about "the God who made the world and everything in it" (Acts 17:24) exemplifies this approach.

There has been a conflict for centuries between evangelical and Roman Catholic theologians over natural theology and arguments from natural law. As Professor Mathew Lee Anderson has recently written in *Christianity Today:*

> Evangelicals have been wary of natural law arguments. As heirs of the Reformation, most evangelical ethicists have argued that the brokenness of human reason makes it insufficient to successfully persuade people in public on the basis of universally accepted moral norms.[96]

Nevertheless, there is more dialogue and agreement now between conservative Protestants and Catholics over powerful arguments from natural theology and natural law to fundamentally build faith in God—and in keeping with the theme of this book, to philosophically define marriage.

A brilliant article appeared in the Winter 2010 edition of *Harvard Journal of Law and Public Policy,* written by Sherif Girgis, Robert George, and Ryan Anderson, which has, according to Professor Anderson, "momentarily managed to reframe the public discourse around a nagging question: what is marriage?" He further observes:

> There may be signs that the frost on the relationship between evangelicals and the natural law tradition is melting—or at least the discussion between the two schools of thought is heating up...Differences between the two traditions will remain. But the willingness among evangelicals to be challenged by the precision and reason of the natural law tradition is a hopeful sign for the renewal of evangelical political thought.[97]

The Rational Understanding of Marriage

So what can a philosophical and reasoned analysis of marriage itself tell us about the nature of same-gender unions and heterosexual marriage?

To carefully and philosophically examine natural law, we must limit our discussion to the study and rational analysis of the definition of marriage among heterosexuals. If the observable nature of heterosexual marriage differs radically from the nature of homosexual "marriage," then their natures will tell us their own unique story about whether these two lifestyles are equal and deserving of equal legal recognition. What does the purely rational and philosophical study of the nature of heterosexual marriage tell us?

CHANGING THE CANADIAN DEFINITION OF MARRIAGE

In February 2005, the Liberal government under Prime Minister Paul Martin wanted to change the historic definition of marriage in Canadian law. The original law defined marriage as "the union of a man and woman to the exclusion of all others." The Liberals felt this could be amended according to the national Charter of Rights and Freedoms to give all same-sex couples their "civil rights" as outlined in the charter, enabling them to "marry" their gay or lesbian partners just as opposite-sex partners could.

The Liberal government didn't examine or try to clarify the original definition of marriage to see what made it distinctive, but simply focused their arguments on the question of human rights and civil equality in order to change the definition of marriage to include the union of any two people. For this government, the debate over same-sex marriage was entirely a question of "charter rights," as they said over and over again on the television news, a matter solely of civil equality. When an issue consists entirely of civil rights, then what any one group has, another similar group also has a right to have. But is heterosexual marriage entirely "similar" to homosexual unions?

This government didn't look to questions of religion or morality in the debate, but only at the question of whether or not homosexuals have equal rights with heterosexuals under the Charter of Rights and Freedoms. They saw marriage as only what the secular state has constructed as a civil institution. If nothing more lies behind marriage than the union of two partners united in heart and mind with whatever sexual relations they wish, then the state, being obligated by the charter to treat everyone in the same way, is not bound by religion or moral arguments from granting any two people their civil rights.

That is what the government of Canada sought to do in recognizing and granting marriage to homosexuals. Hence, by a majority of one vote in the Canadian Parliament, on June 28, 2005, they made what might appear to some to be a slight change to the definition of marriage: from "a man and a woman" to "two people."

Princeton Professor Robert George: A New Focus

The debate on same-sex marriage which the Liberals in Canada treated mainly as a matter of civil rights has gone much further in the last few years. The focus of the debate has now completely changed, partly thanks to a profound article in the Winter 2010 edition of the *Harvard Journal of Law and Public Policy* written by three scholars from Princeton University. What Princeton professor Robert P. George and his two colleagues did was to reframe the question of same-sex marriage, usually based on civil rights, into a much deeper question as to the very definition and nature of heterosexual marriage itself.

In Canada, the definition of marriage was changed from "the union of a man and a woman" to "the union of two people." This appears logical and appropriate if the only issue is the question of equality and civil rights, as many courts of law and international governments have accepted. What the homosexual community received in 2005 was acceptance and equal treatment as couples equal to heterosexuals, thus finding inclusion and recognized equality with everyone else in Canadian society. Some aspects of this, like acceptance and inclusion in society, are of course laudable—but was redefining marriage the right decision based on the observable nature of traditional marriage? Couldn't recognition, acceptance, and inclusion of gays' and lesbians' legal rights be achieved in a better way than by destroying the original definition of marriage?

The much more crucial question at stake here, more than the question of civil rights, is the clear, observable, and comprehensive understanding of marriage itself. If we dare ask the question, "What exactly is the overall, predominant nature of marriage behind the definition of 'the union of a man and a woman,'" what do we find? What are the chief, comprehensive features of traditional marriage? And what is the overarching shape of such marriage, if any?

The Canadian government, acting in 2005, didn't define and analyze heterosexual marriage in their parliamentary legislation—unlike Professor Robert George's careful, thought-through 2010 article that is now creating a seismic shift on the issue.

THE PHILOSOPHICAL DEFINITION OF MARRIAGE

Much more can be observed in the traditional definition of marriage than simply "the union of [any] two people." Most people can observe and find in heterosexual marriages features that make them distinctive and different from any same-sex union. Professor George believes that we can discern by rational analysis the unique features of traditional marriage.

Professor George presents the following definition, based on the common observable features seen in heterosexual marriage that he feels everyone can comprehend:

> Marriage is the union of a man and a woman who make a permanent and exclusive commitment to each other of the type that is naturally (inherently) fulfilled by bearing and rearing children together. The spouses seal (consummate) and renew their union by conjugal acts—acts that constitute the behavioral part of the process of reproduction, thus uniting them as a reproductive unit. Marriage is valuable in itself, but its inherit orientation to bearing and rearing children contributes to its distinctive structure, including norms of monogamy and fidelity. This link to the welfare of children also helps explain why marriage is important to the common good and why the state should recognize and regulate it.[98]

Then Professor George presents what some pro-gay revisionists might view as the definition of marriage that would include homosexuals:

> [Marriage] is essentially a union of hearts and minds, enhanced by whatever forms of sexual intimacy both partners find agreeable. The state should recognize and regulate marriage because it has interest in stable romantic partnerships and in the concrete needs of spouses and any children they may choose to rear.[99]

One of the arguments against accepting the traditional definition of marriage comes from the revisionist comparison of the exclusion of same-gender couples from marriage and the ban on interracial marriage some years ago. They argue that homosexuals can no more change their sexual orientation than interracial couples could change the color of their skin. Thus, just as the prejudice against interracial marriage changed, all the homosexual couple has to do to be included is to change the prejudice against them.

However, allowing people of different races to marry does not change the definition of marriage! It simply adds a greater pool of marriageable people into exactly the same institution as existed before their inclusion. On the other hand, as Professor George writes,

> Revisionists do not propose leaving intact the historic definition of marriage and simply expanding the pool of people eligible to marry. Their goal is to abolish the conjugal conception of marriage in our law and replace it with the revisionist conception.[100]

If same-sex couples cannot be included under the definition of traditional marriage, then they need their own unique definition, suitable to what makes them distinctive but receiving the same civil rights and the same equality under law. If a change in the historic definition of marriage in fact destroys the original meaning, even though the intention is benign, how can this be right?

For two groups to receive equal rights, they must be basically the same thing. Apples are equal to apples but not equal to oranges, although both are fruit. Both same-gender and opposite-gender couples share some common features, but are they equally the same in their comprehensive nature?

Asked another way, can we observe anything different or unique in traditional marriage that is distinct from homosexual unions? Professor George and his two colleagues use an illustration about the comprehensive, overarching, predominant features of traditionally married couples, features that can be rationally observed, that draw a clear and insurmountable difference between heterosexual marriage and homosexual union. It has to do with the act of reproduction, which comes from what they call in the article "organic bodily union."[101]

The body consists of major organs like the heart, the liver, and the pancreas, to help the body function and sustain its life. However, there is one, and only one bodily organ for life, more specifically for the reproduction of life itself, that consists of two people acting outside their bodies but united in one bodily organic union in the conjugal act of marriage. Men and women are by nature "sufficient" for the proper functioning of their own bodily organs, except for one: that is, the function of "sexual reproduction."[102]

> Thus, their bodies become, in a strong sense, one—they are biologically united, and do not merely rub together—in coitus (and only in coitus), similarly to the way in which one's heart, lungs, and other organs form a unity: by coordinating for the biological good of the whole.[103]

Great good for the national state arises from this "generative act" of a couple when it leads to the reproduction of children. However, this reproductive act of coitus can never be achieved by same-sex couples. The journal explains:

> But two men or two women cannot achieve organic bodily union since there is no bodily good or function toward which

their bodies can coordinate, reproduction being the only candidate. This is a clear sense in which their union cannot be marital, if marital means comprehensive and comprehensive means, among other things, bodily.[104]

What about the cases of infertile couples, disabled married partners, or the elderly who remarry? Are these couples not exceptions to the characteristic "generative act" of reproduction, and thus identical to the same-sex couple in their characteristics?

Again, the article gives a very helpful illustration of a baseball team in a league with other teams. Just like some married couples bear children, by analogy there are some teams that win games. There may be some teams that win very few games, and possibly some teams that win no games at all. Because a team wins no games (or an infertile couple, or elderly couple, bears no children), does this means they aren't baseball players at all? Not at all. You don't have to be a winner of games, or a bearer of children, to be a player on the team or to be counted in the pool of truly married people. Every opposite-sex couple has at least the potential for reproduction, and that includes them in the same "true" marriage pool as married couples whose coitus leads to the bearing of children. There is no possibility of the same thing happening for same-gender couples.

The article presents several significant norms for the unions of couples involved in the generative act. These norms are moral values like faithfulness, permanence, and monogamy, which accompany the bearing and rearing of children. Thus marriage, as conjugal and especially related to children, is *as such* a moral institution. As they write:

Thus, the inherent orientation of conjugal union to children deepens and extends whatever reason spouses may have to stay together for life and to remain faithful.[105]

What Harm in Including Gays in Marriage?

The most difficult question for many of us to answer is why the inclusion of same-sex couples in traditional marriage would affect or damage anyone else, especially heterosexual partners. What is wrong with bringing homosexual partners into the dignity of traditional marriage, fully including them in mainstream society and giving them the same moral value as heterosexuals have always enjoyed in marriage?

The day after the Canadian Parliament voted to include homosexuals in traditional marriage, a spokesman from the gay community exclaimed on television: "See, nothing has changed. People are still married. The sky hasn't fallen in. Everything is still the same as before."

Is that true? Will nothing change because of same-sex marriage? It seems like the kind and generous thing to do. But what is, and what do we expect will be, the fallout of such legislative decisions?

The journal article gives three answers.

First, including same-sex couples in the definition of traditional marriage will distort the comprehensive meaning of marriage for many male-female couples getting married. It is the elites in a nation's culture, like the news media, television and movie stars, the universities, the government, and the churches, that shape and define meaning in society. To change the conjugal definition of marriage, with its special interest in the bearing and rearing of children, to a definition that revolves around the emotional bond of mind and heart *changes the meaning of marriage*. The change we can expect is a diminution of the traditional conjugal marriage into the revisionist one of an emotional union without the "necessary norms" of faithfulness, permanence, and monogamy.

Governments serve a vital role in conveying and helping people to find meaning and definitions for public institutions like marriage. To change the definition of marriage to include homosexuals sends the signal of a change in the institution itself and truncates some of its vital meaning—in this case, it redefines an institution from an organic union leading to children with its concomitant moral norms to an emotional bond of two hearts. Professor George observes:

> In other words, a mistaken marriage policy tends to distort
> people's understanding of the kind of relationship that spouses

are to form and sustain. And that likely erodes people's adherence to marital norms that are essential to the common good.[106]

Secondly, the change will "obscure the value of opposite-sex parenting."[107] A number of medical and sociological studies are cited by the authors to sustain their point that biological parents form the best, the most functional, and the most enduring family units, without demeaning other family systems who may even be trying to follow the pattern of traditionally married couples.

Thirdly, the authors write that changing the definition of marriage to include homosexuals will imperil and "threaten the moral and religious freedom"[108] of the proponents of male-female unions, whose beliefs "will increasingly be regarded as evidence of moral insanity, malice, prejudice, injustice and hatred."[109]

It is often the clergy and lay leaders of churches who object to same-sex marriage, and even though they promote the highest moral values in the nation, it is they who will be viewed with abhorrence by many in the nation if the government defines same-gender "marriage" and moves the public to morally accept it.[110] The very leaders of a moral society will be marginalized and abhorred by the public for resisting a social change engineered and legitimated by the government.

The journal article deals with many other relevant issues on the subject and allows the common reader to enter the philosophical debate at a very high but comprehendible level.

Because same-sex couples do not and cannot have the marital constitution of heterosexuals, with their focus on the conjugal act of marriage and bearing children, it would be wrong to include them—even for the highest purposes of civil rights and inclusion in society—in the definition of marriage, due to the damage such inclusion would do to the inherent meaning of marriage and its common values and good, and due to the threat to the moral and religious freedom of its proponents. Instead, fully equal civil rights and inclusion in mainstream society may be accomplished by giving same-gender couples their own definition of their own unions, with appropriate legislation suited uniquely to them.

LEGAL, SOCIAL, BUT NOT MORAL EQUALITY

At this point, can we now give an initial answer, from our clear and comprehensive research of Scripture and reason, as to how gays can be reconciled with many Christians in conservative and evangelical churches? Three levels of acceptance of homosexuals are at stake here: legal, social, and moral equality, the first two of which many evangelicals may be willing to grant.

The first level of acceptance is legal equality. Many theological conservatives would be willing to grant to any same-gender couple the right to register their relationship with the state with their own rites of passage so they would qualify for social benefits given to heterosexual married couples, including the rights to share in pension benefits and inheritance; the right to recognition of roles in health care; the same rules for settling custody battles as govern heterosexual couples; and property rights at the dissolution of the legal relationship. (Incidentally, this legal recognition was the substance of the amendment to the bill considering same-sex marriage in Canada by the Conservative Party of Canada.)

Laws for legal equality could be modeled after those applied to traditional marriage, with the rules of only one partner at a time and the exclusion of family members, although these conditions might be considered as only arbitrary measures without the same binding need as required in heterosexual marriage. Legal equality could use a distinct name, such as "same-sex unions," or "same-gender covenants," to recognize the distinctive nature of homosexual relationships.

The second level of acceptance is social equality. Many have felt that this acceptance can only be gained through marriage itself, giving full social equality with heterosexuals. One of the major concerns for homosexuals comes from seeking to be socially accepted, a recognized part of society, included within the structures of family, church, culture, and the commercial media, wanting to come out to their society as distinctive but also as sharing the need for acceptance and meaningful relationships. The liberals in the Christian churches have seen no other way to achieve social equality for homosexuals than by giving them full equality in marriage and leadership in the church, as is given to celibate singles and traditionally married clergy.

However, many conservative Christians can, and want to, give social recognition and equality to gays and lesbians without granting marriage or ordination. Evangelicals can be very good neighbours to gays and lesbians living on their streets, treating them with acceptance as people deserving of respect. Other forms of social equality and acceptance can come from Bible-believing Christians, who can relate to, appreciate, and value the loveable gay characters in situation comedies on television, their distinctive roles in movies, and especially the stars we see as guests or hosts on radio and television talk shows. We can accept homosexuals as talented people, and in many other ways as moral people. It remains a mistake to think that the only way that Christians can give social equality and acceptance is through marriage and ordination.

Gays and lesbians seek a third level of acceptance through what can be described as *moral equality*. And here is the true sticking point. Theological conservatives cannot grant moral acceptance or "equality" to sexually active homosexuals, whether single, living together, or married, since gay marriage can never be viewed as true, biblical marriage, nor as a morally defensible lifestyle. Any sexually active same-gender person has the same moral standing as a sexually active single heterosexual, or as the opposite-gender couple cohabiting before marriage. Evangelicals steadfastly defend the marriage of one man and one woman as the only venue for sexual activity according to God's voice in the Scriptures. The push by revisionists for gay and lesbian marriage to attain all three levels of legal, social, and moral equality with everyone else in the culture, all through the one institution of marriage, has been immense, and it remains their passionate goal.

Yet we have seen that the rational analysis of marriage yields the same results as the clearest and most comprehensive interpretation of Scripture. Together, they help to answer the fundamental question we asked from the beginning: "Are sexual relations outside the marriage of a man and a woman acceptable according to the revealed will of God?"

OPINION POLLS HAVE CHANGED

The most recent national polls of the general public in both Canada and the United States show that a majority of the population now supports the marriage of same-gender couples based mainly on arguments from equality and civil rights. Political leaders are very sensitive to public opinion and do frame legislation in light of these views. Believing churches may have to separate their view of same-sex marriage as a civic institution from their view of its morality. If the federal government in the United States, as did the government in Canada, were to legally allow gays and lesbians to marry, this would neither change the evangelical view of marriage nor affect evangelicals' views about what they affirm as God's will for sexual relationships. Conservative Christians can live in a country that allows same-sex civil marriage while still faithfully honoring their views based on Scripture and natural law.

What we have presented in this chapter is not a demand for any nation to impose the morality of Christian churches on all its citizens, but a request that nations act in a fair way to make equal things equal and to respect the intrinsic differences between traditional opposite-sex marriage and same-sex unions which require two different definitions, and thus, two different names.

While some conservatives are willing to compromise in giving legal equality, and many have hearts willing to show social equality and acceptance, there may remain theological obstacles when the evangelical Christian is confronted with unrepentant sexual relations between same-sex persons, notwithstanding marriage itself. For the conservative believer, this awkward position is the cost of faithfulness to Scripture and the price we pay for witnessing while still reaching out in many other loving ways to gays and lesbians.

Even though the state may allow homosexuals the same rights of marriage as heterosexuals, the church cannot and does not need to do the same. While the laws of the country may be liberal, based on a policy of secularism and the attendant issues of civil rights, Christian denominations must base their decisions on both the correct interpretation of

Scripture and the philosophical, rational study of traditional marriage. Thus the church must necessarily draw different conclusions to the question of same-gender unions than what the state may choose to accept.

Different Definitions Required

Our rational study of the nature of heterosexual marriage and homosexual "marriage" has shown that they are not the same thing. Opposite-sex marriage is a oneness of a man and a woman with the distinctive potential for the biological reproduction of children and the rearing of these children, calling for the values of faithfulness and commitment of the parents for stable family life, which then contributes to the overall good of society. Same-sex "marriage" can never be brought within this definition since it can never involve the biological reproduction of children by two parents and it will never include the rearing of any children by two opposite-sex biological parents. These are major distinctive differences calling for separate definitions of these sexual "unions."

To include both heterosexual marriage and homosexual marriage under one inclusive definition, as Canada has done in changing "a man and a woman" into "any two people," loses the original strength of the definition of marriage. We are left with a homosexual friendly but ultimately impoverished concept. Does heterosexual marriage have the same features as homosexual marriage, as is implied by the new definition? Will heterosexual couples wanting to share their future lives together still value marriage, and want it, if marriage is given the same meaning by this new definition as homosexual union? If marriage no longer has a distinctive meaning for heterosexuals, what will happen to families, to their children, and to their children's children? And will there still be the same attraction to getting married at all if marriage appears to have a gay definition of merely a union of like hearts and minds?

From a civil standpoint, we need two distinctive definitions if both types of union are to receive recognition. They are different and must be defined differently. In secular society, giving a separate definition for same-sex unions and opposite-sex marriage allows both to appear as legally equivalent, and in the eyes of the revisionists, to have equal moral value. However, we must also recognize that this will never completely close the gap between those who approve homosexual union and those who do not. For the church, the only legitimate marriage is that of a man and a woman, as approved in the trajectory for marriage in Scripture and evident in the argument for marriage from nature, while the sexual relations of same-sex couples, notwithstanding their "marriage," do not receive the approval of Scripture but everywhere find disapproval. The state can legislate same-sex "marriage," but the government can never make it the same as heterosexual marriage, which alone receives the legitimization of most Christian churches.

NATURAL LAW AS PREEVANGELISM IN THE MARRIAGE DEBATE

Evangelicals question the fundamental faculty of the "natural" person, controlled and inhibited by sin, to find the truth on his own without the help of the Holy Spirit. Although natural theology and natural law can lead the unbeliever and seeker in the direction of God and toward the truth about Christian ethics, the final authority must be God, the Holy Spirit, who alone can remedy the malady of humankind's sinful nature achieved in the life and work of Jesus Christ.

Albert Mohler, president of the Southern Baptist Theological Seminary, had an insightful discussion with Professor Robert George on his radio program about George's landmark article. At the end, President Mohler observed, "I'm thankful that he's making [these arguments] better than just about anyone else is making them. And as an evangelical, we have every reason to use natural law arguments; we just don't believe that in the end they're going to be enough."[111]

For evangelicals, the huge benefit of both natural theology and natural law comes from their intellectual power for preevangelism, helping unbelievers to find faith in God or to accept the legitimacy of ethical laws. These rational arguments for marriage and theism from nature do not deal with the problems of human sin and cannot provide the answers for forgiveness and eternal life discovered only in the life, death, and resurrection of the Savior Jesus Christ. However, they do strongly further the argument for righteous beliefs and actions and can be of immense value to a secular society which attempts to find rational answers to questions like gay and lesbian marriage.

Homosexual marriage is nothing more than a creation of the civil state. Yet while this discrepancy may always leave some awkwardness between married homosexuals and the structures and ordinances of the church, creating what many see as "the uncomfortable church," there must always be acceptance and love of everyone as a person created by God.

Pro-gay author Andrew Marin regrets when the church sees that it "has no choice but to fight the gay community,"[112] as Marin sees evidenced in some ex-gay authors.[113] Marin is looking for Christians to show openness and dialogue with GLBT people. However much this is necessary, it still doesn't erase all the difficulties between sexually active homosexuals and evangelicals who may long to witness to, steadfastly love, and pastorally care for gays and lesbians.

The church wants to reconcile with GLBT people. But how do we cross what may still appear to be an apparently hostile barrier? What more do we have to offer than legal and social equality? That question may best be answered in the next chapter as we look at the pastoral care that can and should be given to the gay and lesbian community.

Chapter 7

Pastoral Care of Gays and Lesbians

W hen Ellen DeGeneres became a spokesperson for JC Penney, a conservative group called A Million Moms protested and asked parents to boycott their stores, claiming Ellen, as a lesbian, was unfit to be a representative to their children. This resulted in an outpouring of very bad press against conservatives, suggesting that those against homosexuals are narrow, bigoted, and hateful compared to the tolerant and loving moral majority of those supporting gays and lesbians.

The charges aren't completely without merit. What in the world has happened to evangelicals in their attitude and ministry to homosexuals? For some reason, many conservatives in the church are completely off their game plan when dealing with GLBT people. The most loving people I have ever met are Bible-believing Christians in evangelical churches. But somehow their relationship with homosexuals has been hostile, even offensive, and has brought harsh criticism from the media and the public generally. What has happened here?

When I was a student at New College, University of Edinburgh, in 1971, a church historian observed that the early Christians in the first three hundred years in the Roman Empire won their place as the dominant religion because they:

- outthought the pagans,
- outloved the opposition, and
- outdied their persecutors.

Today, it appears that only a small remnant of evangelicals fall within this orbit of the early Christians. So often the preaching in evangelical churches on sexuality is nonexistent, or of no help at all, or just offensive to gays, not realizing how sensitive they are to being different, how some cry themselves to sleep because of what they feel is their unchangeable orientation and wake up each morning feeling the same way they prayed the night before would be taken away from them.

The intense isolation and suffering of gay men is well documented in current books on the subject. Yet some in the so-called believing churches picket gay parades in what appears to same-sex partners to be outright assault and hatred. Sometimes fathers in evangelical families will throw their sons or daughters out of the family in an effort to change their behavior, which only intensifies their pain and sense of worthlessness. Students at school or coworkers on the job sometimes joke about gay and lesbian orientation and humiliate their colleagues, making them feel not just different, but like they are a terrible mistake of God.

As the author of this book, I realize that even the Scriptures referring to sexuality can be used as weapons against hurting people who want to be accepted and loved like everyone else, not to be angrily pushed away by overzealous evangelicals. Scripture is called the sword of the Spirit of God, meant to help the church combat error and misguided personal opinion, but it is not to be shot aimlessly as a poison missile to embitter and drive away the very people it intends to guide and win to faith in the Savior.

Again, constantly we must remember the apostle Paul's admonition to speak the truth in love. Without our giving gays respect and acceptance as regular human beings, the Scriptures we quote will only hurt and not help to heal. The exegesis of Old and New Testament passages on the subject is unceasingly crucial for the church, but it also demands a commitment to friendly dialogue and a positive attitude toward homosexuals, whom we find to be, in so many other ways, moral people.

In that spirit, this chapter will describe the pastoral care the church can give to homosexuals, not just in the help groups of bigger congregations, but in smaller congregations as well.

Reverend Joe Dallas, as an ex-gay minister, writes as a powerful advocate for evangelical ministry to homosexuals. He offers this powerful observation under the heading, "Where Is the Real Help?"

So the homosexual is caught between two voices: the liberal and the conservative Christian, both of whom are repeating part— but only part—of Christ's words to another sexual sinner, the adulterous woman:

"Neither do I condemn you; go and sin no more" (John 8:11).

"Neither do I condemn you," the liberal theologian comforts today's homosexual. "Go and sin."

"I *do* condemn you," the conservative Christian too often seems to retort, "so go and sin no more!" Or else he just says, "Go!" The sinner is then left alone to figure out just how to "sin no more."

No wonder the gay Christian movement looks so appealing to the woman or man struggling with homosexuality. It offers them acceptance and understanding that they may never have found in the church.[114]

How did conservative Christians get so off their game plan into acting so wrongly? How do we break out of this cycle of criticism, verbal abuse, and intense hurt, or what many gays observe as just plain irrelevancy, especially with those who are already in our churches? If the statistics according to the website of Focus on the Family are correct, that 2 to 3 percent of people in the general population are homosexual, what does that mean to the local church with one hundred members? Statistics say there are two or three GLBT members already in that church, struggling desperately with same-sex attraction and maybe also wanting to live a Christian life.

GAY CHRISTIAN RIGHTS

Before presenting the type of ministry needed to remedy this, let us ask what brought us to this point of hostility or blatant neglect in the first place. A brief look at the history of the gay rights and the gay Christian liberation movement will show us how the church took such a bad turn on this issue.

There has always been a flourishing subculture for gays and lesbians in Europe and North America, and before the twentieth century it broke into mainstream society at times. We can think of the unmatched beauty of the classical music of Pyotr Tchaikovsky, or the brilliant wit of playwright Oscar Wilde, and how their flourishing, hidden gay world emerged into celebrated international fame. Little changed in the first half of the twentieth century, although there were a few seminal books on the subject, like *Homosexuality and the Western Christian Tradition* by Anglican theologian Dr. Derrick S. Bailey in 1955, which began the reinterpretation of the Bible's references to homosexuals, and a 1963 pamphlet by the Society of Friends (the Quakers) promoting the moral equality and acceptance of homosexuals.

Those of us who are baby boomers remember our heady university days in the 1960s and 1970s of love-ins, sit-ins, anti-Vietnam demonstrations, and the rise of the marijuana and LSD drug culture. During this period, the American Medical Association was reflecting upon and reframing their views on homosexuality, recognizing it in 1968 as a natural expression of sexuality and no longer a disorder requiring therapy.

Little did many of us know about the impact the 1969 Stonewall Riots in New York would have, touching off and igniting the gay rights issue, which very soon was to be championed in mass media as the "slavery issue of our time." It seems the riots began when police raided a bar, possibly known as a gay bar, for selling liquor without a license, arresting a few patrons and ejecting several hundred others onto the street, which resulted in rioters throwing stones at the police. These riots continued for several nights.

These riots, at the Stonewall Inn in Greenwich Village, may have been completely overshadowed by the other major news stories that year—like Woodstock, the first man on the moon, and the Manson murder trial in California—but these public riots by hundreds of gay men and women over that week in June 1969 were to change the mentality of the world about gays and lesbians. From the public seeing homosexuality "as a condition or a behavior, it was now to be considered as a fundamental part of one's makeup, no less permanent than skin color or gender," Dallas observes.[115] These riots would also serve to galvanize the militancy of gay rights marches around the world.

Things were rapidly and unalterably changing. Dallas comments:

> By shifting the focus of homosexuality from behavior to identity, the gay rights and gay Christian movement gained new ground by "gradually turning" as Goode explains, "what had been a series of sexual sins into an identity, a way of being."[116]

The issue didn't stay out of the church. What started as the gay civil rights movement, a child born of its times, quickly began to take on a religious identity as the gay Christian movement, which in turn gave increasing legitimacy and support to secular gays and lesbians.

The founder of Metropolitan Community Church in Toronto, Reverend Brent Hawkes, told me in an interview that "gay rights has been the wedge issue" behind the march of homosexuals toward full equal rights with heterosexuals. However, Christian churches were becoming involved in the campaign so that the gay rights movement morphed very powerfully into the gay Christian movement, offering full moral Christian equality with heterosexual marriage and the ordination of gay ministers.

What began as a demand for recognition and acceptance in secular society was now finding legitimacy in some Protestant churches. A special impetus came from the founding of the Universal Fellowship of Metropolitan Community Churches by Reverend Troy Perry in 1968. There are now three hundred UFMCC congregations around the world, ministering to gays and lesbians and their supporters in a very eclectic Christian worship service. Brent Hawkes did not see his Metropolitan Community Church in Toronto as a branch of the Christian church, but as "a breakaway" Christian community.

The theologically thin glass façade of many mainline Protestant denominations was beginning to crack. First the United Church of Canada and then the Anglican Church of Canada gave their support to gay marriage and ordination. In America, the Episcopal Church, the Presbyterian Church (USA), the United Methodist Church, and the

Evangelical Lutheran Church of America all saw pro-gay advocacy groups rise and flourish in the 1990s and beyond. In 2003, the Episcopal Church in America ordained the Reverend Gene Robinson, an openly gay cleric, as bishop, and in 2011 the Presbyterian Church (USA) ordained their first gay minister.

Newspapers, television, and the movies have crusaded endlessly since the 1990s for gay liberation and kept the fires of civil rights fiercely burning in many news stories and newscasts. The courts voted again and again for equal rights for gays and lesbians, and then the Parliament of Canada in 2005 picked up the cause as a national legislative issue and barely squeaked it through the House of Commons to make homosexual marriage equal to heterosexual marriage. At the time of this writing, President Obama has indicated that he no longer supports only "civil unions" for gays and lesbians, but now supports the civil rights of homosexuals to have marriages fully equal to heterosexual marriages.

CONSERVATIVE CHRISTIANS REACT

During all this, where were the conservative Christians in the Protestant denominations? It should be noted that up until today, the majority of voting commissioners in the Presbyterian Church in Canada and in many other denominations in Canada and the United States have not supported the moral approval of gay marriage or ordination. A majority have held to the traditional interpretation of Scriptures dealing with sex and marriage. However, there is a constant attrition among the numbers of conservatives in this war over homosexuality. Many of North America's best seminaries and their professors are teaching theological students seeking ordination the revisionist view of Scripture on marriage and sexuality.

What began as an isolated protest against exclusion and persecution gained terrific momentum as a drive for the goal of equal rights. The pro-gay movement found support from some Christian denominations that legitimized homosexual sexual identity and sexual practices and took them to the next level of moral equality in both marriage and leadership in the church. Having now achieved their earlier goals, activists are advancing into the schools to educate young students about their sexual identity and are touting the power of their "unstoppable" movement to change all the institutions in Western culture, not excluding all the main-line Protestant denominations.

On the positive side for conservatives, there have been strong advocacy groups in many denominations in Canada and the US, like the Renewal Fellowship within the Presbyterian Church in Canada, that have published scholarly reports and testimonies supporting the traditional view of marriage and ordination while often making very constructive cases for ministry to homosexuals.

While many Protestant denominations still have on their books very uplifting and biblical statements on everything from love, marriage, and godly celibacy for singles to prohibitions against cohabitation, promiscuity, and homosexuality, they rarely proclaim it from their pulpits, and even more dispiriting, they have no idea how to minister to those homosexuals who are already in their churches, let alone those who never pay any attention to the church. Those special days focused on love, such as Valentine's Day, Christian Family Sunday, or Father's Day, are an opportunity for pastors to speak on their denomination's policy on sex and marriage. The address can be especially suited for the youth, also keeping in mind the parents and grandparents who influence them. What authority pastors have when representing to their congregation the official policy of their denomination, and, to the contrary, what a disaster if their denomination has changed, or worse yet, has no official stance on matters of love, sex, and marriage! In those cases, the minister must speak solely from his own position on the subject.

In those congregations where the denomination has changed its doctrine on homosexuality, the minister can speak on celibacy and virginity for the unmarried, and sexual faithfulness for those married, when celebrating a special marriage anniversary or on Sundays like the one around Valentine's Day, by upholding the many examples of those heroes in the Bible who best represent biblical marriage. The minister can avoid interjecting personal opinion, which might not be well received, by quoting and making his point from the godly illustrations in Scripture.

The very first thing every Christian in every church should remember in our relationships with gays and lesbians is to emphasize greatly the phrase in the middle of Paul's highest ethical teaching: "Love never fails" (1 Corinthians 13: 8).

If you have ever lived in a neighborhood where you sometimes meet a gay couple, you already know what it means to love. We must never be less than civil, decent, and kind in our attitudes. We do this to everyone else (or at least we should), not just to those who may be of a different religion from ours but even to outspoken opponents of all religions. That kind of respect and decency is not hard; in fact, it's common to almost all of us.

All the churches I have served as pastor have been very loving fellowships, where every visitor entering the worship service will receive a warm welcome at the door and a love-in during our greeting just after the service begins. If we Presbyterians can do this, having been called "God's frozen chosen" for so many years, every congregation can foster this kind of warmth progressively. Whatever the impression of the evangelical sermon preached that day, at least visitors will know the love of those around them!

A more proactive approach can be taken as well. A number of large congregations offer help groups for those suffering from same-gender attraction, within which individual Christian workers give personal support, encouragement, and accountability to those seeking help. When ministers announce self-help groups, they should be both sensitive and bold enough to include a kind invitation to those in their church who want to deal with same-sex experimentation.

When a Married Gay Couple Comes to Church

Conservative pastors should personally reach out to do everything within their denominational standards they can for gays and lesbians. Let me give a brief illustration of this from a true story—which is also depicted on the cover of this book—of something that can and does happen in conservative churches today.

In a church I served, our best attended service of the year was always the candlelight carol service on Christmas Eve. The single son of a couple in our church would come only once a year, to that service. I welcomed him for several years, and on the third year, as he came out the door he said to me, "I want you to meet my partner." Then another young man came out after him, whom I warmly welcomed to the church and sincerely thanked for coming.

The next year, the parents of this man, who were very faithful, believing Christians, invited me to a birthday party at their home where the two adopted sons of this now married gay couple were celebrating the children's birthdays. In asking me, the grandparents were tentative and seemed to want to give me an opportunity to gracefully turn the invitation down. This family all knew I always preach a biblically centered sermon.

I immediately told them that my wife and I would be delighted to attend the birthday party. I would never turn away from an opportunity, even one out of my theological comfort zone, to represent the Christian church and possibly share the gospel of the Lord Jesus Christ! I was aware that the gay couple had been married under Canadian law and that gays could legally adopt children.

At their home, I found a huge backyard tent with streamers and balloons everywhere. The grandparents had come from a Catholic background, and a very large contingent of family, friends, and neighbors were in attendance. There was a ton of food on the tables.

When I saw the food, I immediately wondered if the grandfather of the children, whom I knew to be a very committed Christian, would ask me to say the blessing over the food. Actually, I anxiously longed for him to ask me, because I saw a tiny opportunity where I could have a ministry to the gay couple, their two children, and all their guests. He did ask me.

I remember that prayer:

"O God of all families, I thank you for the gift of love and faithfulness that started with the grandparents of this family. Please bless Sean as he tries to be a good father to these boys. Keep Frank faithful in his commitment to the boys as well. Let these two children know discipline, faith, and love in their lives, so they can become the kind of men you want them to be. And, O God, it is our prayer on this beautiful day that everyone in the world will have food to eat and fresh clean water to drink as we give thanks for this wonderful food. In Jesus's name we pray, amen."

There were about one hundred people there who said a loud amen with me, and then they all broke into enthusiastic applause. They didn't hear me support gay marriage, but they were delighted and relieved for me to lead in a prayer that they too wanted to give, a prayer for the support of families, for the children, for the joyful birthday celebration, and for all the good food.

I realize that not every evangelical minister would be able to go to this birthday party, because a person's presence does give a message of support and approval all its own. But in the gospels, Jesus went into compromising situations all the time—like talking to a forbidden foreign woman all alone who was living common-law with her sixth husband (John 4:1–38), or accepting the expensive anointing and the kissing of his feet and washing them with her tears by a known sinful woman at Simon the Pharisee's home (Luke 7:36–49), or the blatantly scandalous visit to a known thief and robber's home for a free lunch in Jericho at the home of Zacchaeus the tax collector (Luke 19:1–10). Jesus risked disapproval for the very reason he gave in his mission statement at Zacchaeus's home: "For the Son of Man came to seek out and save the lost" (Luke 19:10). Should believing pastors fear going anywhere where they could share the gospel?

I could do this ministry in good conscience because I didn't need to bless the gay marriage; I asked God's blessing on the two men separately in the parental role—whether I agreed or not, whether I liked it or not—that they were given by the government to raise these two young boys. Children should always receive the fervent prayers of the church.

The two men thanked me separately later at the party and said they were grateful I was willing to come. Ministries like this open doors for people to come to church, where they will hear how to find and know the Lord Jesus Christ personally—and where they may hear God's call to repent. I feel we must never put in jeopardy our opportunity to witness to gays and lesbians through angry or hurtful remarks or actions, but should always do whatever ministry we can to keep an open door to lead them to the Savior and to God's own timing for them to repent and live a godly life.

I believe it is biblical to give gays and lesbians the social space they need to feel free to make their own decisions. That is what the father of the prodigal son gave to his son in Jesus's parable; the father didn't issue his son an ultimatum or throw him out of the family because of his desire to leave. The father, a picture of God the Father, helped his son to be free so he could even choose to leave home, despite heading toward a life of dissipation and ruin (Luke 15:11–32).

Prodigals need to be free to find their own place in society to do what they feel they want to do. This is not a time for critical censure and hurtful actions and angry words from evangelical families and people in the church! When they are given their space to be what they want, hopefully that space—and the patience and loving witness to the gospel needed to go with it—will lead the prodigal back home to the love of the heavenly Father.

We can and must witness to the clear teachings of Scripture and the arguments from a rational definition of marriage in the courts of law and in the governments, but we should never try to force upon GLBT people our views when they are not ready to listen or deny them their freedom to do what they want to do. Despite whatever we try to do to prevent their going down that path in the first place, they must be free to do what they choose for themselves. The imperative that believers in Christ always face becomes visible in the loving gospel welcome when God works in their hearts to bring them home. And God fulfills his promise that his Word does not return void. This can be seen in the stories of those who do repent and return home, as in the testimony of two ex-gays in the next chapter.

What about giving approval to pro-gay churches, or to the Christian pastors' associations that include gay ministers? This is another question altogether, because here the question is not one of loving and accepting gay people so much as it is one of supporting an agenda that is not ultimately helpful to those people. The Reverend Joe Dallas, an ex-gay man who has come out of churches such as the Metropolitan Community Church, says he would never support any church where gay and lesbian people will not hear the true gospel about God's revealed will for all human sexual relationships. In this, it is well worth our time to listen to him and others like him as they share their stories and help us better understand how to minister to the GLBT community.

A Gay Church Service

When I recently attended the Metropolitan Community Church in Toronto, I saw a very eclectic worship service. As a prelude, the piano and drums were playing Broadway hits. Like in the Anglican Church, the clergy processed in carrying a cross with two lit candles. The vestments of the clergy were like what you would find illustrated in Lutheran liturgical catalogs, with the colors of blue, gold, and white, and the embroidery of a shepherd's crook. They claimed a very traditional Presbyterian dash when the beadle carried in an open Bible and placed it on the lectern. In the middle of the service, the foot-tapping anthem could be taken from the gospel music you would hear in a Baptist church. The cantor led in psalm-like choruses, not unlike what you would hear in the Roman Catholic Church. The sermon taught social justice, like you often hear in United churches. Personal prayers for individuals in attendance, with the anointing of oil on the forehead, gave a blessing like you might find in a charismatic church. They had a very traditional prayer of confession with an assurance of pardon, like you find in many Protestant churches. And the closing "Hallelujah" was the current hit by pop star Leonard Cohen, leaving attendees with a bit of a Jewish flavor.

But I also saw men partners and women couples, young and old, who wanted to be there together. I didn't know how long they had been together or how faithful they were to each other, but I had a sense they had found a spiritual home in the worship service that morning. I had the sense that something helpful might be happening, somehow. Why would I think that, if all they hear is the reinforcement that homosexuality is acceptable to God and they never hear the truth of the gospel so as to repent and find a godly life?

I knew there were some things wrong with what I saw. Yet I had a feeling that I could not minister to all these people in the same way that this church can. Maybe this is how the prodigal tries to worship in the distant country—risking, by worshiping there, the danger of lacking deep repentance and costly forgiveness, and raising the critical question of whether the prodigals will ever find their way back to the Father's home. I thought maybe the breakaway MCC church or a revisionist Anglican/Episcopal church can do something I'm unable to do for GLBT people, by accepting them as equals and giving them an uncomplicated welcome.

Yet the homosexuals I saw at MCC are not the whole story. Another large group does seek to know God and to live according to the Bible within an evangelical context. In the next chapter, we will encounter two gay men who were able to change their same-gender attractions and live victorious Christian lives, giving us profiles of homosexuals that evangelical churches can clearly see and positively relate to.

But what about the large majority who cannot change? Can they find saving faith and some measure of ongoing sanctification in the breakaway and revisionist churches? While this could in some way be true, what a complicated and risky ministry homosexuals may find in the pro-gay churches! My greatest hope for those in these churches comes from the reading of the Bible in their worship services. I know the power of the Scriptures, for as St. Paul wrote, "I'm not ashamed of the gospel, for it is the power of God for the salvation of everyone who believes" (Romans 3:16). The reading of the Bible is more powerful than any misinterpretation of it. It always remains "the power of God for the salvation of everyone who believes"! Whenever the Scriptures are read, it gives me hope for people hurt by a hostile world, seeking solace and peace on a Sunday morning in a worship experience which may have some Christian elements.

Should mainline churches follow the lead of revisionist churches such as MCC? Ultimately, while these revisionist churches may appear to have some benefit and appeal for homosexuals, they also forfeit something priceless in doing so. They may never win back the right or the authority to help the nation find God's will for the biblical celebration of sex and marriage. The immediate gratification of revisionist ministries to homosexuals could end up paying unending losses in failing to guide the young men and women of the nation into the lifelong process of finding faithful, strong, monogamous, opposite-gender marriages. This cost appears to be far too great for any Christian denomination to risk paying. Breakaway and revisionist churches may offer temporary comfort and hope as a home for homosexual worship, but the long-term damage in the nation to abstinence, sex, and marriage might never be repaired. For this reason, mainline Christian denominations must never compromise their biblical confessions on homosexuality in such a way that would blur or confuse God's will for sex, marriage, and ordination.

Some mainline denominations have minorities wanting to have their own breakaway congregations, with freedom to conduct same-sex marriage and hire a practicing gay staff person—expecting the national church to allow it in the same way as liberal elements of unbelief have been tolerated and accepted in the church for decades now. But it must be remembered that despite departures from church doctrine by some clergy in pastorates or seminaries, their theological views have almost never been reflected in the confessional statements of the church. Christian denominations can have only one statement for their doctrine on human sexuality. They cannot allow some congregations to follow one part of an ethical statement on homosexuality while other congregations follow other elements in the same report. While such diversity might reflect real differences existing within the denominations, passing recommendations would lead to conflict within the courts and among the leadership of the denomination, resulting in a completely subjective misinterpretation of the Bible and the loss of authority for the denomination to speak as the body of Christ. Such a theological cleavage would mute and eventually eliminate the prophetic voice of the denomination not just on one issue but on the credibility of the entire gospel itself, possibly fueling an ecclesiastical schism as well.

Study and debate on homosexuality in the Presbyterian Church in Canada reached its culmination in the Special Committee Re: Sexual Orientation report to the 2003 General Assembly in Guelph, Ontario. Their report raised many questions, but one of their fifteen "Further Thoughts" in the report was the following:

> The position of the Presbyterian Church in Canada on this subject is also unambiguous. The 1994 "Statement on Human Sexuality" adopted by the 120th General Assembly (A & P 1994, p. 252–74), reaffirmed the biblical and traditional view that: "Committed heterosexual union is so connected with creation in both its unitive and procreative dimensions that we must consider this central to God's intention for human sexuality. Accordingly, Scripture treats all other contexts for sexual intercourse as departures from God's created order." In light of this stance, and in recent precedence, The Presbyterian Church in Canada is not prepared to ordain unrepentant practicing homosexuals or to allow public worship services blessing same-sex relationships.[117]

Accordingly, the General Assembly passed the report recognizing "the distinction between sexual orientation and homosexual activity,"[118] the former permitting an individual to serve in any capacity, while the latter, when the candidate is a self-declared practicing homosexual, barring the candidate from being ordained or married in the church. Even with some dissenting voices, strength and stability come from this clear declaration that earlier assembly reports founded so powerfully upon the Scriptures. Thus the nation can know the mind of Christ from the church speaking by the Holy Spirit in the Scriptures. It was our Lord Jesus Christ himself who warned his disciples how crucial it is to obey and keep his words in Scripture:

> Everyone then who hears these words of mine and acts on them will be like a wise man who builds his house on a rock. The rain

fell, the floods came, and the winds blew and beat on that house, but it did not fall, because it had been founded on rock. And anyone who hears these words of mine and does not act upon them will be like a foolish man who built his house upon sand. The rain fell, and the floods came, and the winds blew and beat against that house, and it fell—and great was its fall!

MATTHEW 7:24–28

North American culture now finds itself in the midst of a torrential storm of moral antinomianism and religious relativity. Our house of faith will surely suffer that great fall if we don't faithfully obey the words of the Lord, and his Holy Spirit, in Scripture!

We have examined the pro-gay churches and their uncomplicated welcome to homosexuals without any requirement for change. Should the Christian church accept GLBT people without any expectation of change, or should we accept them with the goal of seeking a life transformation found by grace through faith? Let's look now at our mission field, and to those who have made significant life changes in their sexual orientation.

Chapter 8

HERE IS THE MISSION FIELD

M any conservative churches are unable to effectively reach out to gays and lesbians who visit their congregations, much less offer to start a ministry to people struggling with same-gender attraction, even to those who may already be in their church.

It's easy to lay all of the blame for this on mindless Christians, but there is some fault on both sides. The problem for many evangelical Christians, when trying to relate to homosexuals, comes from the gay public persona seen at gay parades and through men kissing each other on television or in public. Most Christians could never see morality in some of the costumes and near nakedness in the annual gay parades. And when gays say they are "proud" of these displays of risqué behavior, it results in feelings of moral outrage for many Christians who may truly want to be conciliatory (and possibly also for some of the more respectable homosexuals themselves).

Evangelicals may want to love the people in these displays, but they cannot accept so much of what they see that the public persona creates emotional barriers and moral indignation, making acceptance and the hope of any kind of ministry impossible. In the rest of this book, I want to help my fellow evangelicals break through these sexual stereotypes to see some real people toward whom we can envision real ministry and acceptance.

EXODUS INTERNATIONAL

Like many Christians, I struggled with the stereotypes seen in the media and at gay pride events. The breakthrough for me came in the fall of 2010, when my wife and I attended an Exodus International regional conference in Endicott, New York. There, we heard a number of compelling testimonies from ex-gay and lesbian Christians who had worked through their immense sexual struggles to reach heterosexual marriage or chaste singleness. As I listened to their stories, for the first time I could finally see who the homosexuals were! Each person was distinct and diverse, but they all had feelings for the same sex that they were working through.

It is far more difficult to see the real people in the gay parades or the media façade of homosexuals. Here were people just like me, but with real struggles and strong feelings that were different from mine. I could immediately accept these persons as true Christians, people who wanted desperately above all else to live a biblical life. And they had what evangelicals could quickly recognize and positively relate to as "victory in Jesus" in their lives. These were real people I could talk to and minister to. They also gave me and others a powerful incentive to reach out to gays and lesbians outside the church, as we were able to see and hear in the ex-gay testimony the temptations and painful struggles they had, just like so many others we meet today who don't know Christ and the power of his name.

People with homosexual struggles represent a very real and endearing mission field. In this chapter, we will discover how two men found help with their same-gender sexual desires. Their lives can stand as a call to compassion from evangelicals, as well as showing the way to effective ministry. The first is a minister, John Howard, from Barrie, Ontario, Canada; the other is Exodus International executive director, Alan Chambers. Both men offer us hope for ministering to others who are like them—real people with relatable struggles.

John Howard has given permission for his story to be quoted here in its entirety. He calls it "A Pastor's Story."

Growing up, I was always the smallest kid in my class, and was very self-conscious about it. Mom made it worse by always begging me to eat bigger meals. "John, look at all these people staring at me," she whispered to me one day on the bus. "They're wondering why I don't feed you more." Although she really loved me, she unwittingly contributed to my feeling that there was something wrong with me. When I was 13, my father got a job transfer from Calgary, Alberta to Thunder Bay, Ontario. That was a rough transition for me. I was just starting high school, and it was frightening.

The first day in my new school, a guy named Bill invited me to his church. I'd gone to Sunday school sporadically, and knew it would be a good place to find some new friends. So I started going every week with him to the church just down the hill from our school. Later, in grade 10, we were invited to a six-week series of classes, to be followed by a special confirmation service for those who wanted to join the church. I'll never forget the sermon that Sunday morning. "You're not joining a club," the minister told us. "What you're really doing is giving your lives to Jesus Christ, asking Him to come in and take control." I'd never heard that before.

"God," I prayed, "if You're really there, I invite you to come into my life. Please forgive me for my sins, and help me become the person You want me to be." As I prayed, something happened. Deep inside I just *knew* that God was real, and I was overwhelmed with the feeling of being loved. God loved *me*, little John Howard! It was amazing! After that service in April, 1963, I went to every possible church activity. I had a new hunger to read the Bible and pray. God and church suddenly became a very important part of my life. By grade 12, I sensed God wanted me to become a pastor.

But at the same time, something else was happening, something hidden and troubling. As a young teen, I discovered a pile of old sporting magazines down in the basement. Flipping the pages, I was drawn to the Charles Atlas Ads. Looking at the muscular body-builders, I thought *Now that's what a real man looks like. I wish I could look like that.* I found those photos sexually arousing, and started masturbating while looking at them. Later, I accidentally discovered another magazine in a corner store, filled with handsome men in swimsuits and jock straps

131

in seductive poses. I felt fascinated and turned on. I felt guilty for looking, and yet the sexual excitement was strong and powerful. Thus, an inner conflict began that would continue over 20 years. On the one hand, I prayed that God would take away these feelings; on the other, I continued to find them enjoyable. I was too ashamed to tell anyone else what was happening inside me.

I had a lot of girlfriends during high school and felt very comfortable around them. Despite the increasing sexual desire for guys, I assumed I'd eventually get married. Through school and church, I met a girl named Vicki and we started dating. We married when we were both 21, but the conflict inside of me only increased. Often, I'd have homosexual fantasies while being intimate with my wife and secretly sought out magazines and books to feed my homosexual desires.

Posted to our first church in 1972, Vicki and I had our first daughter, and then adopted a son. Later, we had another girl. I deeply loved my wife and children, but the lustful thoughts were out of control. Although I didn't want to lose my family, I felt an increasing desire to act out my homosexual feelings, to see if reality was the same as fantasy. In the summer of 1974, on my way home from a conference, I was delayed and missed my connecting flight in Winnipeg. Instead of staying with friends, I went to a hostel which had the reputation for homosexual activity. Another man approached me that night, and I invited him to my room. After he left, I headed for the showers. I felt so guilty and dirty—and afraid of venereal disease. Later that night I knelt beside the bed and prayed. "God, I'm so sorry. Please forgive me. I'll never do this again! Please take away these feelings!"

Years later, on staff at a large church in Barrie, Ontario, frequently I had to travel to Toronto, attending meetings and doing hospital visitation. On these trips I had trouble staying out of adult bookstores. "God, please help me," was my frequent prayer on those drives into Toronto. But once I got there, it felt like a huge hand pulled me in. I'd browse through the gay magazines and memorize the pictures, later fantasizing about what I'd seen. I felt angry and guilty—but I couldn't stop. Then I started driving past cruising areas and reading graffiti on bathroom walls. I knew if this behavior continued, I'd get drawn into homosexual activity again. If that were to happen, I knew I'd eventually get caught and lose my family and my job. I saw destruction down that path.

Meanwhile at church, I was meeting regularly with ten small group leaders. Discussing problems in their groups as well as any personal issues, we got to know each other really well. One Friday after a meeting, Anne and Merle approached me. "John, we sense you're really struggling with something," they said. "If you ever want to talk, we want you to know we're here for you." I brushed them off. "Oh, no, everything's fine. Thanks a lot." Inside, I was scared. "Now they can see I'm homosexual!" I thought.

The following Wednesday, I ended up in an adult bookstore in Toronto. On the drive home, God spoke to me: "John, I've provided these people for you to talk with." I called one of the ladies that night and said I needed to meet with them. The following Friday, I talked to them all afternoon, pouring out my soul. They loved and accepted me, often crying with me as we shared together. We committed ourselves to meeting every two weeks. Each time, we asked God to tell us what we needed to be discussed, and then waited for Him to reveal an incident or feeling to talk and pray about. Gradually we uncovered the roots of my behavior and God began the process of restoration in my life.

These women became my support group and my accountability partners. When I was going to Toronto, I could call them up and ask for prayer. What a difference! The "hand" at the bookstore was now puny and withered, and I could resist it when I wanted to. The addiction to pornography and masturbation began to wane. God showed me that my sexual addiction had become my way of comforting myself in hurt, anger, stress, loneliness, and boredom. He began to teach me how to handle those emotions in a healthy way. He also helped me to accept my body, to realize that it was His gift to me, not something to be ashamed of. He brought healing to my fractured relationship with my father, and He gradually helped me feel confident in my masculinity and my identity as a man.

The restoration that took place in that year was huge for me! While for over 20 years I had begged God to work a miracle in my life *supernaturally* (without anyone else knowing), God had a different way. He wanted to use *people* to help restore me. He was applying the truth of James 5:16, "Therefore, confess your *paraptoma* [trespasses, sins, flaws, faults] to each other and pray for each other so that you may be healed."

After about a year, I knew my wife had to know what was going on. One night, I finally confessed to her my struggles with homosexuality. Vicki was hurt that I'd kept this part of me from her for so many years, but she affirmed that she had married me "for better or for worse." As long as I was seeking healing, she would stand beside me. But if I ever went out and had another affair, whether homosexual or heterosexual, that would be the end of our marriage. Her healthy boundaries helped me to want not to fall again. And, I slowly discovered that we could enjoy each other sexually *without* my needing a homosexual fantasy for stimulation.

The healing process continued over the months (and is still going on—He's not finished with me yet!). One morning in 1983, on the news I heard about the arrest of a group of men in another city for homosexual activity in a public washroom. After they were booked and released, one of them, a man who'd been a Sunday school teacher and elder in his church, returned home to say good-bye to his wife and children, then went out and killed himself. I wept, knowing that, except for God's grace, that could have been me. "God," I prayed, "I give You permission to take my story public if it can prevent even one person from taking his or her life."

It was amazing how God started bringing people across my path who told me about their struggle with same-gender attraction. I eventually started a support group, and was asked to be on the Board of New Direction, a Christian ministry whose mission is "to create a safe place for same-gender attracted people to journey toward wholeness in Christ." Since 2006, I've been working as a counselor. I love my work helping men, women, youth and their families come to terms with same-gender attractions, learn how to handle them in healthy and non-destructive ways and discover how to manage and change addictive thought-processes and behaviors and to enjoy becoming the people God intends us to be, free of guilt and shame.[119]

There is immense value and importance in ministry to people like John Howard. How we treasure people like the women who were in John's support and accountability group! And we can take heart from the underlying truth of the story that ministry to homosexuals is not futile. No matter how long-kept the secret of same-gender sexuality, the fact that people who struggle with this will respond to the offer of support, a listening ear, encouragement, and the loving presence of other believers should affirm to us the validity of this ministry, which could be endorsed by even the most conservative churches.

Do homosexuals have to change in order to visit a Christian church? Despite different theological positions, all Christian denominations know that when strangers visit a worship service, they are to be welcomed unconditionally. They don't have to pass anyone's standards of morality or achieve any demands for good works to sit in church on a Sunday morning, possibly hearing the minister expound on the apostle Paul's words in Ephesians 2:8–9: "For by grace you have been saved by faith, and this is not your own doing; it is the gift of God—not the result of works, so that no one may boast."

That gift of God's Son mentioned in this verse, the Lord Jesus Christ, with his atoning death and resurrection, does not come with a price tag—it's all free! This is not just "cheap grace" but entirely *free* grace! What cheapens this gift is the immense inertia against moving the new believer along the path toward sanctification. John Howard received the free gift of God's grace in high school, but it wasn't until years later that he sought his church's help to deal with a sexual problem that was threatening to destroy his family and his career in the church.

SENSITIVITY TO THE MISSION FIELD

The mission field for ministry to homosexuals is immense, and when the "natives" in what appears as a "foreign mission field" do come to church on a Sunday morning, the faith community must be ready to welcome them with a loving introduction to the free grace of the Lord Jesus Christ. Nothing must ever put in jeopardy, either by critical words or unkind actions, this opportunity to minister the word of life, grace, and salvation to perishing souls who come seeking for God in our congregations. We must leave to God the place and time of their call to discipleship to follow the Lord in a godly life. It may take a lifetime of repeated repenting after repenting to achieve success in living a righteous life.

Another great testimony of a young man struggling with homosexuality is that of Alan Chambers, the current executive director of Exodus International.

Alan became a Christian at the very early age of six years. But even from that early age, he didn't feel comfortable as a boy. "The constant unsettled feeling of not measuring up to what was expected as a boy—and a Christian one at that—was nearly too much for me to bear… because of my deep fear of rejection and even retaliation, I ended up bearing that great burden all alone through almost my entire childhood."[120]

Alan remembers his mom as an exemplary Christian woman whom he tried in every way to imitate. On the other hand, he tried to be totally unlike his father. His father was a military man, completely unpredictable in his mood swings from kind father to utter bear. Alan recalls: "While I only received about three memorable spankings from Dad, it was his day-to-day anger and roller-coaster moods that taught me early that I didn't want to be anything like him or be anywhere near him." His dad loved shopping and cars but could verbally rip Alan to shreds in a department store. "By the time I was six I hated Dad and vowed I would never be anything like him. He was the meanest man I knew."

However, Alan's father wasn't his only abuser. In fourth grade his fellow students teased him mercilessly, and sixth grade was the "worst year of my life" with taunting, name-calling, and constant bullying. Then Alan writes: "And to top off a pretty unhappy childhood, like so many others, around age ten I was molested by an older teenage boy."[121]

Alan retreated into a fantasy world and enjoyed playing the role of a girl. From age three or four he sorted through his sister's clothing closet and dressed as if he too were a girl. "I learned to escape into a world of make-believe. In that make-believe world, I was a girl...While I wanted to be a girl, I knew I wasn't and that I couldn't ever be one. It was a tortured life."[122]

Alan felt different from his brothers and the other boys at school. "By the time I entered sixth grade, the difference earned me the label 'gay.' Sadly, but finally, my difference had a label." Alan tried to take the road toward acceptability with his peers. He pretended to like things he didn't; he developed an incredible sense of humor. Then, as he had conversations with gay men, he wanted to have what they had. *"Homosexuality might be wrong, I often thought, but how will I know it won't meet that aching need inside my heart if I never try it?"*[123]

Alan writes of going to a gay bar and how he felt "strangely at home."[124] He returned to the bar the next night with dreams of its exciting possibilities. He called it "the hunt."[125]

"Going to the bars was my feeding ground, and men were my prey. I loved preparing for the hunt...it was invigorating and exciting. The fantasy of what I would find was intoxicating. I couldn't wait to live it... More hunting. More sex. More fantasy. More masturbation. New ways of achieving all of it. I was definitely addicted. And I had lost something precious—and I knew it. My desire to be accepted—and to accept myself wasn't happening either."[126]

Evangelicals often have negative thoughts about homosexuals

"coming out," thinking it only gives social reinforcement to an immoral lifestyle. However, it's necessary to come out in order to face your true self and your need to publicly change. Alan writes a powerful passage on coming out as a gay man:

> And when people can't stay in the closet any longer and they "come out," it's often less about sex than it is about their sense of being. Again, people say they are coming out of the closet as "gay," but they are really coming out in a much deeper sense. Their God-given gifts and talents and personalities come out too. These things that they hated in themselves, thanks in part to gender and cultural stereotyping, emerge. For instance, my decorating skills were no longer a secret. The real coming out for me involved getting out of homosexuality and accepting who God truly created me to be. I came out of my denial that I was created to be a man...I came out of self-hatred of being a touchy-feely man who could cry easily and be hurt. I came out of the fear of showing my real self to people. Their opinion didn't matter in light of what God thought about me and what I thought about me.[127]

Alan's first great breakthrough came at an Exodus International Freedom Conference at a Kentucky seminary when God spoke to him to reconcile with his dad, who might be hurting as much as Alan was. He then went back to his dad and began a new start of forgiveness and reconciliation that over the years has deepened into great respect and love. His dad had also become very faithful in attending church. Alan remembers: "Forgiveness caused a refreshing rain to fall on the desert of my heart and turn it into a lush garden of love, grace and mercy. I believe I truly became a man when I forgave my dad."[128]

Alan, now twenty years old, was attending the Exodus program called Exchange with other gay men struggling with their sexual desires. Exchange urged the men to go beyond group counseling to find an accepting church fellowship. Alan was "struggling with whether or not I was going to keep fighting homosexual desires or chuck the agony and completely embrace the gay life."[129]

Then something remarkable happened, which at first may seem insignificant but which launched a radical change for Alan. When dropping off some food at his sister-in-law's, she bluntly asked him, "Are you more attracted to men or women?" Alan awkwardly stuttered for a minute, and then she answered that it was okay however he would answer. She said she cared about him and that she would love to have him attend her church with them. She mentioned there were many people struggling with homosexuality who were able to overcome it. That night he went with her to Discovery Church in Orlando, Florida. He felt the same excitement going to that church that he felt the first night he went to the gay bar, and he hoped it would be a life-changing experience. And it was!

He went Sunday morning, Sunday evening, and on Wednesdays. He loved the music, the messages, and the people who embraced him. In particular there was a man called Kirk, a "guy's guy," married, the father of three, an athlete and a leader, and he liked Alan. I want to quote the next four paragraphs in his book, *Leaving Homosexuality,* at length, because they show another portrait of how the conservative church can identify with and know what it means to minister to homosexuals:

> Not too many weeks into my time at Discovery I had what they called a "Ministry Time" with Kirk and the other leader. Kirk led it. He basically asked me to share my hurts. What a thing to ask!
>
> I poured out my heart. I shared hurts related to being angry with my dad. I talked about being ridiculed and made fun of by my peers. I confessed hurt over not being liked by my brothers or even feeling accepted by them. All of this got to the core of my gaping and deeply infected wound of needing a man to love me, which sure was something that fueled my struggle with homosexuality. I remember craving the simple nonsexual touch and embrace of a man and spending hours fantasizing about such encounters. I had wanted that since I was very young. And

I know some of you reading this can relate.

Confessing that need reduced me to a bawling heap. And that's when something I never would have imagined happened. Kirk reached out and embraced me. It wasn't premeditated or contrived. It was like a father reaching out for his son. It was my heavenly Father reaching out for me. Kirk hugged me and I sobbed. In Matthew 5:4, one of the beatitudes says, "Blessed are those who mourn, for they will be comforted." Never had mourning felt so good to me.

I'd never felt such comfort from a man…from a father…as I did that afternoon. I spent many hours crying with Kirk and the other leader that day. Kirk spent the time simply letting me weep on his shoulder. It was one of the most satisfying times of my life. Even now, as I remember that day, I feel a centeredness and peace and comfort. It was so remarkable! I knew it was God the Father hugging me through this man.[130]

Very quickly Alan came out to everyone in Discovery Church and to all his family. He says it wasn't a big deal for the people in the church, "because the people at that church categorized all sin the same way… here my homosexuality was just another item on the list of what Jesus could heal."[131]

Alan continued to struggle with sexual temptation but gained more and more victory. There is a testimony at the beginning of his book that I would like to include:

You probably have some hard days—I know I still do. But I have peace and joy amid those difficult times like I never dreamed possible. I wouldn't go back to homosexuality for anything… no, not for *anything!* I wouldn't trade what I have now (the Lord, my wife and my kids) for anything the gay life has to offer. Been there, done that.

Not too long ago Friday night rolled around and I had on my fat clothes (you know—elastic-waist shorts, big T-shirt, glasses only worn around the house with people who love you). We'd eaten pizza from a local Italian restaurant, the kids were bathed, Leslie was propped up on the couch, and it was almost DVD time. I said to her, "This is the life I treasure. It's my dream come true, and nothing could ever tempt me to leave it or you or them or my Jesus."[132]

HELP IS AVAILABLE

These remarkable testimonies from John Howard and Alan Chambers can help conservative Christians to unmistakably see their mission field. While revisionist and breakaway churches integrate homosexuals into their fellowships without requiring or expecting any change in their sexual activity, more conservative evangelical churches can hold out hope for God's Holy Spirit to change a gay or lesbian's sexual desires in God's own time and with the support, encouragement, and loving presence of God's believing people in the church. Although some gays can successfully undergo sexual conversion through restoration therapy, such as these two men did, others can be empowered by God to live a chaste, single life with victory over their sexual urges. The Presbyterian Church in Canada has a moving closing section in the Church Doctrine Committee's Report on Homosexual Relationships that must be considered in conclusion here:

Is "No" the only word that the Church has for those who struggle with homosexuality? To be merely negative is lacking in pastoral sensitivity. The Church must listen to and share the very real pain of homosexuals and their families. While we cannot ignore the direction of Scripture, at the same time we cannot minimize neither the human pain or the potential of homosexual men and women; nor can we ignore our Scriptural calling to witness to God's love of all God's people and the power of grace.

God has so created us that we humans need each other. Social intercourse is necessary for all. Sexual intercourse, however, is not. Life can be full and abundant for the single, both homosexual and heterosexual, without sexual intercourse, despite the dictates of current society. Sexuality, which is inherent to all of us, can be expressed in other ways than by genital activity—in friendship, in affection, in touch and in belonging. The alternative is not between the intimacy of homosexual intercourse on the one hand and the pain of isolation and repression on the other. The Church is called to be a welcoming, nurturing, loving and supportive community, a true church family, where all are welcomed, nurtured, loved and supported. Sadly, the Christian Church has frequently shunned homosexuals and failed to minister with them and to them. The Church as a whole must repent of its homophobia and hypocrisy. All Christians, whether our sins are of the spirit or of the flesh, whether heterosexual or homosexual, need God's forgiveness and mutual forgiveness as we pursue together the path of holy living. Grace abounds, and in our weakness God's strength is made known.

Some will refuse our call for homosexual chastity as impossibly idealistic, or reject it as psychologically unhealthy. Sexual chastity, it is argued, is a gift, and not everyone with homosexual orientation has this gift. However, the grace offered by the Lord Jesus Christ is neither cheap, allowing us acceptance without repentance, nor is it powerless. The Gospel contains within it not only the demand for transformation but the power to achieve it.[133]

So if gays and lesbians are to be reconciled with the church, how can we summarize the terms of peace? What can gays and their revisionist supporters expect from the conservative, believing church? That conclusion comes next.

Chapter 9

THE TERMS OF PEACE:
THE FUTURE OF GAYS IN THE CHURCH

I n Luke's version of the Great Commission in Acts 1:8, we read, "You will be my witnesses in Jerusalem, in all Judea and Samaria, and to the end of the earth," and the church has always been that—individually through missionaries and collectively through the prophetic pronouncements of national denominations. It is the God-given nature of Christian denominations to speak out to citizens and national leaders on many ethical and theological issues.

Each year, the General Assembly of my own denomination sends a loyal address to the prime minister assuring him, and all parliamentarians, of our prayers, as well as letters to government ministers expressing our opinion on political matters. This is considered the prophetic voice of our Christian denomination. Also, some of our doctrinal statements get picked up by the secular media and are broadcast to the nation. Along with the single voice of the brave Christian missionary, this ecclesiastical voice of the denomination fulfills the calling to be "witnesses...to the ends of the earth."

What happens if the denomination loses its legitimacy and hence its authority to witness to the gospel and reveal God's will on moral and theological matters? How can the people of a nation find guidance for their lives when the church can no longer be heard or listened to? A nation without guidance from God loses its sense of right and wrong and declines into an antinomian collectivity. The Bible tells us this in Proverbs 29:18: "Where there is no prophecy, the people cast off restraint."

Old Testament Turbulence

National turbulence is no stranger to the Bible narrative. The tale is told again and again: evil king, evil nation; good king, good nation; true prophets, good guidance; evil prophets, moral decay. The history book of 1 Kings reveals in its two closing chapters the perils of false prophets leading the king and his people to national disaster.

Let us recall the conflict of the prophet Elijah with the wicked King Ahab and his wife Jezebel, whose name is synonymous with corruption and evil, and especially the showdown of Elijah with the 450 prophets of Baal on Mount Carmel. Ahab, in constant conflict with Elijah, wanted to kill him. He called him a troublemaker in Israel because Ahab never received a favorable answer from the prophet. Ahab supported the 450 prophets of Baal (the male fertility god of the surrounding pagans), and Jezebel funded the 400 prophets of Asherah (the female fertility goddess). Their destruction of true Jewish religion is legendary, and they stand as some of the worst monarchs of all of ancient Israel.

In the last chapter of 1 Kings, a national decision regarding going to war—allied with their neighboring better half, the southern kingdom of Judah—had to be made. King Jehoshaphat of Judah, a relatively good king, visited Ahab of Israel to discuss a possible alliance in war against neighboring Aram to recover their lost city of Ramoth-gilead.

Jehoshaphat was devout enough to ask King Ahab to consult with the prophets to see if victory could be assured. Ahab's false prophets quickly announced, "Go up; for the Lord will give it into the hand of the king" (1 Kings 22:6). But Jehoshaphat had enough common sense to seek the council of a true prophet of God like those in his homeland of Judah. Here is their conversation in the Bible:

> The king of Israel said to Jehoshaphat, "There is still one other by whom we may inquire of the Lord, Micaiah son of Imlah; but I hate him, for he never prophesies anything favorable about me, but only disaster." Jehoshaphat said, "Let the king not say such a thing." Then the king of Israel summoned an officer and

said, "Bring quickly Micaiah son of Imlah"…The messenger who
had gone to summon Micaiah said to him, "Look, the words of
the prophets with one accord are favorable to the king; let your
word be like the word of one of them, and speak favorably." But
Micaiah said, "As the Lord lives, whatever the Lord says to me,
that I will speak."

When he had come to the king, the king said to him, "Micaiah, shall we go to Ramoth-gilead to battle, or shall we refrain?"
He answered him, "Go up and triumph; the Lord will give it
into the hand of the king."

1 KINGS 22:8–15

Surely this was all Ahab needed: a true prophet of God to chime in
with the four hundred false prophets of Asherah. However, there was
something about the mockery and irony in Micaiah's voice that disturbed
the mind of Ahab on this. The literary note in the NRSV *Harper Study
Bible* offers this insight:

Micaiah then prophesies that Aram would win the battle. One
would suppose that Ahab would have heeded the word of the
true prophet of God. Instead he made light of Micaiah and said
to Jehoshaphat that his message was to be expected from one
like him. Micaiah then went so far as to answer that God had
put a lying spirit in the mouth of all of Ahab's false prophets. It
is hard to understand why Jehoshaphat, who had some spiritual
insight, did not then and there divorce himself from Ahab and
go home without joining the fray.[134]

Tragedy followed: Jehoshaphat joined Ahab in battle. Ahab's strategy
was to disguise himself as a common soldier so the Arameans would not
single him out and pursue him. This might have been successful except
that a soldier from Aram shot a random arrow into the sky, and the Lord
God of Israel guided it "between the scale armor and the breastplate" to
mortally wound the king (1 Kings 22:34). By nightfall Ahab was dead,

fulfilling the prophecy of Micaiah and sending all of Israel into bitter defeat.

The tragedy here comes not just from false prophets, but from having two opposing groups of prophets on different sides giving different advice.

THE PERIL OF CONFLICTING PROPHETS

The story fits the present crisis of the different views of sexual morality in North America. "Who is right?" the elites of the nation ask: the revisionists who help us accept the immense changes in the liberation of homosexuals in our time, or the conservatives in the church who have the backing of Scripture, traditional values, and the theology of historic Christianity? How will our political leaders hear the advice they want to hear from the Christian churches when the leadership of those churches are so divided? How will heterosexuals know God's will for them if the church cannot hold to a credible biblical policy for homosexuals? Which group of prophets will be heard on this matter?

Indeed, God's words that arrested me and drove me to write this book speak as Scripture to everyone in the church today:

If you faint in the day of adversity,
Your strength being small;
If you hold back from rescuing those taken away to death,
those who go staggering to the slaughter;
if you say, "Look, we did not know this"—
Does not he who weighs the heart perceive it?
Does not he who keeps watch over your soul know it?
And will he not repay all according to their deeds?

PROVERBS 24:10–12, NRSV

Micaiah in King Ahab's day summoned all his courage to speak the truth and did not "faint" or shrink from the task of trying to rescue "those taken away to death, those who go staggering to the slaughter," as fulfilled in the person of King Ahab and the bitter destiny of the nation of Israel. However, because there were conflicting prophecies, conflicting views, and conflicting messages presented as being from the Lord, there was no hope of rescuing those who were "taken away to death." Ahab himself was one of the first to fall.

How can the nation know God's will? What group of prophets will speak on God's behalf? There will always be the outspoken pastors on the radio and television, and in pulpits, who will shout their outrage at the immorality of their time. But the national courts of the Christian denominations also have a prophetic voice to speak to the great questions of our time! As in Ahab's day, it is no less urgent today that Christians be faithful and bold to warn and rescue those "staggering to the slaughter"!

We now have the revisionists attempting to accept everything homosexual as morally equal with heterosexuals, and traditionalists wanting to keep the same standard as found in biblical times and during the long eras of the Christian churches. At the same time, we deeply desire to walk in love toward homosexuals themselves. What do we, as evangelical believers, do?

EVANGELICAL TERMS OF PEACE

Here, then, is a summary of "the terms of peace" all evangelicals must consider. Perhaps ironically, revisionists have seen these terms already. I believe many conservatives and evangelicals will be willing to accept them, including accepting many of the historic cultural changes we have seen in recent times for GLBT people:

- A sheer minimum of civility and decency in attitude toward all homosexuals, just like you might give to any other neighbor on your own street.
- The offer by many conservatives to give legal equality and social equality—which may be enough to create meaningful relationships—and thus to compensate for the refusal to give moral equality based on Scripture and according to the comprehensive definition of the nature of traditional marriage.
- A sincere and very warm welcome to homosexual visitors to their churches.

- An acceptance of homosexuals as created by God and having immense value.
- An acceptance of honesty in the church and the opportunity for homosexuals to "come out" so as to tell us who they distinctly are with their unique gifts and personal struggles.
- A caring, supportive, and accountable fellowship of believers in conservative churches to accept those struggling with same-gender desires and wanting to live a righteous life.
- A deep love for those who gain victory over same-gender desires and enter heterosexual marriage or a satisfying celibate single life, viewing them as representative of all homosexuals as a starting point for mission to gays and lesbians, including those who cannot or will not change, and those who are indifferent to the church.

On the other hand, the revisionist and breakaway churches must understand that conservatives in the church will never compromise their view of holy Scripture. That will always remain nonnegotiable, and liberals and conservatives will never find a foundation for reconciliation that compromises the evangelical's view of Scripture.

I have tried to show why evangelicals remain so defiant on the place of Scripture in the homosexual debate: it is because of the deep, abiding Bible-believing culture in which the evangelical is constantly immersed, by reading and studying Scripture daily, and by "praying without ceasing" throughout the day. This biblical culture will not change despite the huge pressure from mass culture surrounding evangelicals, demanding they accept the sociological changes we see happening for homosexuals—and despite the doctrinal changes happening in some mainline denominations, and even in some rare evangelical churches or seminaries.

The liberals need to know where evangelicals stand and should be warned that if a denomination seeks to revise its theological view of Scripture in order to give full equality to marrying and ordaining homosexuals, it will always constitute a huge crisis for the conservatives in the church. It may result in only a few changes to that denomination in the short term, but within a generation or two, those changes will bleed away almost all the evangelicals in that denomination, who tend to be the keepers of the church's reverence for Scripture and the most zealous in church growth and outreach. The church's historic identity and commitment to mission, the lifeblood of that denomination, will be drained away with the abdication of the evangelicals from their churches.

EMERGING SCHISM?

On June 28, 2011, Canada's *National Post* ran an article on St. Alban's Anglican Church in Ottawa, a historic church once attended by Canada's first prime minister, Sir John A. Macdonald, a founder of Confederation and the Thomas Jefferson of Canada. This congregation of three hundred members was leaving the Anglican diocese because of their denomination's acceptance of same-sex blessings.

After the Anglican Church of Canada in 2007 passed the blessing of same-sex marriage, granting the same moral value to same-sex marriage as to heterosexual marriage, a number of congregations made plans to separate from the denomination and ally with the new Anglican Network in Canada. St. George's Anglican Church, also in Ottawa, had already separated before St. Alban's.

St. Alban's was founded in 1865, two years before the federation of several provinces to form Canada. As the *National Post* reports:

> "This is kind of historic. We're in a new era," said Sheila Lang, 79, as her grandchildren—the seventh generation to attend the church—played in the reception hall of the Ottawa Little Theatre, where the congregation, now called the Church of the Messiah, will meet until it finds a permanent home...
>
> The move is historic in a broader sense, Ms Lang added: "This is a societal shift," in which traditional Christian values are "eroding and we see the church trying to accommodate the eroding values.
>
> "But we are not deviating—We stand on the Bible and the word of God."

Reverend George Sinclair [the minister] urged the congregation not to dwell on grief over losing St. Alban's, but instead to embrace the change as an opportunity for change.

"We are entering a time of new drama and new visions," he said on the stage of the theatre, flanked by reproductions of three stained-glass windows Macdonald's wife donated to St. Alban's after his death.

The minister said the immediate catalyst for the church's break from the diocese was the Anglican decision to accept same-sex blessings. *The National Post* reports:

Rev. Sinclair added that his church was also responding to a general sense that the Anglican Church of Canada has been drifting away from Jesus' teaching.

"If you end up thinking you're smarter and nicer and wiser than the master, in what way are you still his disciple? The Bible is very clear on certain things, as to what is right or wrong," he said.[135]

How does a congregation like this make a decision to leave its denominational roots, which have nourished them over so many years? The Christian church in all its diverse denominations has few authoritative resources to go by in its historic and contemporary decisions and proclamations. Primarily, it possesses the Old and New Testaments of the Holy Bible; secondarily, it has the sources of the Bible's interpretation and the confessions of faith and creeds in its two-thousand-year tradition. Any radical departure from these authorities undermines the well-being and the life itself of the church.

Same-sex blessings and moral approval of same-gender marriage and ordination lie on the surface of a much deeper malaise of unbelief in some seminaries and in some pulpits, especially emerging from the time of the European Enlightenment in the eighteenth century. For some Christians, the Enlightenment is not just seen as a time of the flourishing of music, art, and culture, but also as the beginning of the dark ages for philosophy and theology as intellectual atheism emerged, a movement that can be dated from the fall of the Bastille during the French Revolution in 1789 and which we are only now recovering from with the fall of Communism and the Berlin Wall exactly two hundred years later.[136]

The problem of unbelief—with its strong origin in the Enlightenment—lies at the heart of the problem with the church today. Warnings have been issued to the Christian churches like the one given to the Anglican Church of Canada by their own international evangelist, the Rev. Dr. Marney Patterson. He fired a shot over the bow of his eroding church in his 1999 book *Suicide: The Decline and Fall of the Anglican Church of Canada*.[137] Marney pointed out that between 1965 and 1995, 954 churches were closed in the Anglican Church of Canada, but more alarmingly, between 1992 and 1994, 526 Anglican churches were closed in Canada. Reverend Patterson singled out, among other issues, the acceptance of common-law and same-sex unions as signs responsible for the decline. Marney told the *National Post* on July 17, 1999, that "disgust with this decline of standards is one of the main reasons many Anglicans have left the denomination for evangelical churches."

Alarm bells are ringing for conservatives in mainline and evangelical Christian churches today. The liberals in these denominations need to know exactly where the Bible-believing members stand. This book attempts to explain where I believe many conservatives stand, and it presents the mutual ground that evangelicals can invite the liberals to take with them in reconciling gays and lesbians to the body of Christ.

In closing, I have no desire to impair the vision or weaken the moral protest of evangelical churches on this issue. Conservatives see some clergy in the mainline Protestant denominations valuing love as the greatest power and highest theological virtue in ministry at the expense of sound biblical theology. Because of this, evangelical clergy may be apprehensive in offering unconditional, loving pastoral care to homosexuals, feeling that they risk changing their beliefs through a compassionate ministry to GLBT people. That risk will be best handled if pastors and their congregations keep faithful to the Word of God, correctly interpreting the Christian Scriptures, as they wholesomely reach out with biblical pastoral care.

The case has been made here that loving pastoral care must be combined with theological faithfulness to offer the Christian church's truly unique gospel to a troubled world. To be extreme only on the pastoral or prophetic side could isolate a minister or denomination from the wholeness of Christian identity in what was called by the early Christian fathers "the holy, catholic, and apostolic church."[138] Living on the extreme margins of the Christian identity loses the balance and wholeness of the Christian faith.

Rather than loving pastoral care, evangelicals have often chosen abrasive quarrels with unrepentant, practicing homosexuals. These Christians have operated in their biblically prophetic role of declaring God's judgment on all sins, but they have done so most emphatically on the sins only of homosexuals. This is neither deserved nor honest to the Scriptures. Harsh public demonstrations and protests broadcast by the media do not at all help the evangelical witness to the gospel or their ministry to homosexuals. While it is not my intention to weaken conservative churches by eviscerating their prophetic voice, it remains equally important that we not turn away from loving pastoral care because of the risks of contamination by an ungodly world or an overanxious fear of theological compromise.

All North American denominations would excel at their calling by combining the prophetic voice of protest and warning with loving pastoral care in the way summarized earlier in this book by the apostle Paul: "Speak the *truth* in *love.*" To combine *truth and love*—pastoral care and prophetic pronouncement—is always a demanding and risky business, but our Lord and Master Jesus Christ not only everywhere exemplified this, but compels his disciples to do the same!

Can the Protestant churches succeed in perfectly, or even imperfectly, carrying out this ministry of pastoral care and prophetic witness? Or will these roles of the pastoral and the prophetic always be lost in their battle with each other?

I still have hope of finding this balance in the churches in North

THE TERMS OF PEACE: THE FUTURE OF GAYS IN THE CHURCH

America. Jesus promised in Scripture that he would build his church, "and the gates of Hades will not prevail against it" (Matthew 16:18). I still believe that if we continue faithfully to be the church that the Lord Jesus Christ founded, he will honor and fulfill his promise in our time!

THE ANCIENT COLLAPSE OF CHRISTENDOM

Before closing, I would like to share one last illustration on what the division within the Christian churches could mean if we can't work out together our ministry to homosexuals. It is one of the supreme examples of Christians attacking Christians so that they both fall together. It happened in ancient Constantinople.

For 1123 years of the existence of the Byzantine Empire, its capital, Constantinople, was besieged many times but captured only once—during the Fourth Crusade in 1204. The Latin Roman Catholic Church fiercely attacked their separated but Christian brethren in the Eastern Orthodox capital in Constantinople. The stronger western side of Christendom so devastated this great center of art, culture, and the Christian faith that it became powerless to defend itself against the invasion of the Islamic Ottoman Turks in 1453.

Anyone who has visited Istanbul in Turkey (falsely so renamed, according to the Greeks today, from the original name the Greeks gave for their capital of Constantinople) will fall in love with this city that spans both the European and Asian continents. Here you find the most beautiful mosque in the world, the Blue Mosque. But across the park from this magnificent Muslim worship center still stands an even more beautiful fifth-century cathedral, called since the early days of the Christian Empire *Hagia Sophia*. This was the most splendid house of Christian worship and center of scholarship in the entire world for centuries. However, it wasn't the early pagans who destroyed faith and worship here in *Hagia Sophia*—nor the Goths, nor the Vandals. Constantinople, as the center of the Christian world, was destroyed by other Christians. Author Sepros Vryonis writes in *Byzantium and Europe:*

The Latin soldiery subjected the greatest city in Europe to an indescribable sack. For three days they murdered, raped, looted and destroyed on a scale which even the ancient Vandals and Goths would have found unbelievable. Constantinople had become a veritable museum of ancient and Byzantine art, an emporium of such incredible wealth that the Latins were astounded at the riches they found. Though the Venetians had an appreciation for the art which they discovered (they were themselves semi-Byzantines) and saved much of it, the French and others destroyed indiscriminately, halting to refresh themselves with wine, violation of nuns, and murder of Orthodox clerics. The Crusaders vented their hatred for the Greeks most spectacularly in the desecration of the greatest Church in Christendom. They smashed the silver iconostasis, the icons and the holy books of *Hagia Sophia,* and seated upon the patriarchal throne a whore who sang coarse songs as they drank wine from the Church's holy vessels. The estrangement of East and West, which had proceeded over the centuries, culminated in the horrible massacre that accompanied the conquest of Constantinople. The Greeks were convinced that even the Turks, had they taken the city, would not have been as cruel as the Latin Christians. The defeat of Byzantium, already in a state of decline, accelerated political degeneration so that the Byzantines eventually became an easy prey to the Turks. The Crusading movement thus resulted, ultimately, in the victory of Islam, a result which was of course the exact opposite of its original intention.[139]

The greatest risk of Christians fighting Christians, whether in ancient Constantinople or over the place and morality of homosexuality, could be that we will destroy the opportunity, the integrity, and the authority of any church to speak to the nation on God's plan for love, sex, and marriage. If Christians destroy the legitimate voice of one another, the nation could fall to the mounting invasion of an army of unbelievers and the immoral.

This book, written for those wanting the most clear and compelling interpretation of Scripture and reason on the morality of homosexuality, has hopefully accomplished its task. As we definitively understand the issues of morality and the dust settles around this intense debate, Christians will be able to go out and love, accept, and minister the word of life to homosexuals in the light of God's Word and the rational definition of true marriage.

For the conservative church of today, the right and wrong of homosexuality according to Scripture is the primary, first issue to be resolved. From there, we may learn how to move on to many compassionate and life-enabling ministries and become, for gays, more than just the uncomfortable church. Christians should want to show love and draw gays, lesbians, bisexuals, and transgendered people closer to the Lord and to the body of Christ. Let's end the battle with these terms of peace.

ENDNOTES

1. There is a long section in the book by Professor Jack Rogers, often referred to here, about the "Scottish Common Sense Philosophy" of the eighteenth century that was applied to the interpretation of Scripture. Rogers rejects this common-sense, literal reading of the truth directly off the pages of Scripture. It can be briefly said in reply that there is a clear meaning to many passages of Scripture that are transcultural and trans-historical which must be recognized and accepted as plainly revealed truth. Accepting much of the direct, clear truth of the Bible frees the interpreter from personal subjectivity and human control of God's Word so it can remain the objective words from God. See Jack Rogers, Jesus, The Bible, and Homosexuality: Explode the Myths, Heal the Church (Louisville, KY: Westminster Press, 2006), 30–34.

2. "Gay liberation," *Wikipedia*, http://en.wikipedia.org/wiki/Gay_liberation.

3. The Church Doctrine Committee, *The Acts & Proceedings of The Presbyterian Church in Canada* (Toronto: The Presbyterian Church in Canada, 1985), 31.

4. Jack Rogers, *Jesus, The Bible, and Homosexuality: Explode the Myths, Heal the Church* (Louisville, KY: Westminster Press, 2006) Look especially at chapter 5 in this book.

5. Andrew Marin, *Love Is an Orientation* (Downers Grove, IL: InterVarsity Press, 2009), 178–185.

6. The Church Doctrine Committee, *The Acts & Proceedings of The General Assembly* (Toronto: The Presbyterian Church in Canada, 1985), 240.

7. The Church Doctrine Committee, *The Acts & Proceedings of The*

Presbyterian Church in Canada (Toronto: The Presbyterian Church in Canada, 1994), 256.

8. Ibid., 256–257.

9. Please check out the website of Focus on the Family at www.focusonthefamily/social issues/counseling for unwanted same-sex attractions/.

10. Andrew Marin, *Love Is an Orientation* (Downers Grove, IL: Inter-Varsity Press, 2009), 192–193.

11. Focus On the Family Issue Analysts, "Our Position (Pro-Gay Theology)," *FocusOntheFamily.com,* www.focusonthefamily.com/social issues/social-issues/progay-revisionist-theology/our-position.aspx.

12. Focus On the Family Issue Analysts, "Cause for Concern (Pro-Gay Theology)," *FocusOntheFamily.com,* http://www.focusonthefamily.com/socialissues/social-issues/progay-revisionist-theology/cause-for-concern.aspx.

13. Focus On the Family Issue Analysts, "Cause for Concern (Pro-Gay Theology)," *FocusOntheFamily.com,* http://www.focusonthefamily.com/socialissues/social-issues/progay-revisionist-theology/cause-for-concern.aspx.

14. More information can be found at www.FocusOntheFamily.com and in books by ex-gays, including Joe Dallas, *The Gay Gospel*, and Alan Chambers, *Leaving Homosexuality.*

15. The United Church of Canada at its 37th General Council in 2003 accepted a resolution that said that "homosexuality is a gift from God" ("Homosexuality and the United Church of Canada," *Wikipedia,* http://en.wikipedia.org/wiki/Homosexuality_and_the_United_Church_of_Canada) and consequently will marry and ordain practicing homosexuals. The National Coordinating Group reported early in 1988 to allow the full inclusion of those with same-sex sexual orientation into membership in the church, and any member of the church can serve at any level.

16. The ministry of Exodus International demonstrates the success of homosexuals in leaving this orientation and having well-working opposite-gender marriages. Please see the example of John

Howard and Alan Chambers in chapter 8.

17. *Catechism of the Catholic Church*, #2357 (New York: Image Doubleday, 1997).

18. Joe Dallas, *The Gay Gospel? How Pro-Gay Advocates Misread the Bible* (Eugene, OR: Harvest House Publishers, 2007), 190.

19. Ibid.,190.

20. Tom Horner, *Jonathan Loved David* (Philadelphia: Westminster Press, 1978), 82–125.

21. *The Harper Analytical Greek Lexicon* (London: Harper & Row, 1971), 106, 208.

22. Tom Horner, *Jonathan Loved David* (Philadelphia: Westminster Press, 1978), 82–125.

23. The Church Doctrine Committee, *The Acts & Proceedings of The Presbyterian Church in Canada* (Toronto: The Presbyterian Church in Canada, 1985), 241.

24. Jack Rogers, *Jesus, The Bible, and Homosexuality: Explode the Myths, Heal the Church* (Louisville, KY: Westminster Press, 2006), x

25. The Church Doctrine Committee, *The Acts & Proceedings of The Presbyterian Church in Canada* (Toronto: The Presbyterian Church in Canada, 1994), 252.

26. Jack Rogers, *Jesus, The Bible, and Homosexuality: Explode the Myths, Heal the Church* (Louisville, KY: Westminster Press, 2006), 70.

27. Ibid., 70.

28. Ibid., 71.

29. Ibid., 71.

30. John R. Kohlenberger III, *The NRSV Concordance*, Unabridged (Grand Rapids, MI: Zondervan, 1991), 1221.

31. Jack Rogers, *Jesus, The Bible, and Homosexuality: Explode the Myths, Heal the Church* (Louisville, KY: Westminster Press, 2006), 71.

32. Ibid., 71.

33. Ibid., 72.

34. Ibid., 71.

35. See a recent pronouncement by the Archbishop of Canterbury, Rowan Williams, at www.ABC.net.au/news/2007-12-21/archbishop, 1.

36. It was reported in *The Ottawa Citizen* that a recent moderator of the United Church in Canada, Reverend Bill Phipps, denied the deity and the bodily resurrection of the Lord Jesus Christ. Bob Harvey, "Interview with Rev. Bill Phipps," *The Ottawa Citizen,* October 30, 1997.

37. Even some Reformed rabbis have denied faith in the biblical account of Moses and the Israelites crossing the separated waters of the Red Sea. See Rabbi David Wolpe, *Did the Exodus Really Happen?* (Beliefnet.com/Faiths/Judaism/2004/Did-The-Exodus-Really-Happen.aspx).

38. See the account of the multiplication of food and other "biblical" miracles in a new book by Allison C. Restagno, *Modern-Day Miracles* (Shippensburg, PA: Destiny Image Publishers, 2011), 89 ff.

39. Jack Rogers, *Jesus, The Bible, and Homosexuality: Explode the Myths, Heal the Church* (Louisville, KY: Westminster Press, 2006), 17.

40. Ibid., 59.

41. Ibid., 72.

42. Ibid., 73.

43. Ibid., 73.

44. Ibid., 73.

45. The Church Doctrine Committee, *The Acts & Proceeding of The Presbyterian Church in Canada* (Toronto: The Presbyterian Church in Canada, 1985), 240.

46. *The Analytical Greek Lexicon* (London: Harper & Row), 337.

47. Ibid., 272.

48. *The Pocket Oxford Dictionary* (London: Oxford University Press, 1970).

49. *The Holy Bible, English Standard Version* (Wheaton, IL: Crossway Bibles, 2001), 1 Corinthians 6:9.

50. Jack Rogers, *Jesus, The Bible, and Homosexuality: Explode the Myths, Heal the Church* (Louisville, KY: Westminster Press, 2006), 73–75.

51. John Boswell, *Christianity, Social Tolerance and Homosexuality* (Chicago: University of Chicago Press, 1980), 341, 344.

52. Joe Dallas, *The Gay Gospel? How Pro-Gay Advocates Misread the*

Bible (Eugene, OR: Harvest House Publishers, 2007), 211.

53. Jack Rogers, *Jesus, The Bible, and Homosexuality: Explode the Myths, Heal the Church* (Louisville, KY: Westminster Press, 2006), 74.

54. Joe Dallas, *The Gay Gospel? How Pro-Gay Advocates Misread the Bible* (Eugene, OR: Harvest House Publishers, 2007), 212.

55. Ibid., 212.

56. Ibid., 213.

57. The Church Doctrine Committee, *The Acts & Proceeding of The Presbyterian Church in Canada* (Toronto: The Presbyterian Church in Canada, 1985), 241.

58. Jack Rogers, *Jesus, The Bible, and Homosexuality: Explode the Myths, Heal the Church* (Louisville, KY: Westminster Press, 2006), 75.

59. Harold Lindsell, *NRSV Harper Study Bible, Expanded & Undated* (Grand Rapids, MI: Zondervan, 1991), 1841.

60. Ibid., 1842.

61. Thomas Schmidt, *Straight and Narrow: Compassion and Clarity in the Homosexual Debate* (Downers Grove, IL: InterVarsity Presss, 1995), 96–97.

62. Ibid., 97.

63. Jack Rogers, *Jesus, The Bible, and Homosexuality: Explode the Myths, Heal the Church* (Louisville, KY: Westminster Press, 2006), 76.

64. Richard Hays, Marion Soards, and others dismiss many of the passages on homosexuality in Scripture except for the writing of Paul in Romans 1:18–32. See Jack Rogers, *Jesus, The Bible, and Homosexuality: Explode the Myths, Heal the Church* (Louisville, KY: Westminster Press, 2006), 76.

65. Ibid.

66. John Calvin, *Institutes of the Christian Religion,* Book 1, Chapter V (London: James Clarke & Co., 1949), 277 ff.

67. Jack Rogers, *Jesus, The Bible, and Homosexuality: Explode the Myths, Heal the Church* (Louisville, KY: Westminster Press, 2006), 76.

68. Ibid., 79.

69. *English Standard Version Study Bible* (Wheaton, IL: Crossway Bibles, 2008), 2159.

70. Harold Lindsell, *NRSV Harper Study Bible, Expanded & Undated* (Grand Rapids, MI: Zondervan, 1991), 1655.
71. Ibid., 1655.
72. *The Analytical Greek Lexicon* (London: Harper & Row), 432 .
73. Jack Rogers, Jesus, *The Bible, and Homosexuality: Explode the Myths, Heal the Church* (Louisville, KY: Westminster Press, 2006), 77.
74. Ibid.
75. Ibid., 78.
76. Ibid., 77.
77. Martti Nissinen, *Homoeroticism in the Biblical World: A Historical Perspective* (Minneapolis: Fortress Press, 1998), as cited by Jack Rogers, *Jesus, The Bible, and Homosexuality: Explode the Myths, Heal the Church* (Louisville, KY: Westminster Press, 2006), 78.
78. Jack Rogers, *Jesus, The Bible, and Homosexuality: Explode the Myths, Heal the Church* (Louisville, KY: Westminster Press, 2006), 78.
79. Ibid.
80. Ibid.
81. Ibid.
82. Ibid., 79.
83. Ibid.
84. Joe Dallas, *The Gay Gospel? How Pro-Gay Advocates Misread the Bible* (Eugene, OR: Harvest House Publishers, 2007), 207.
85. Jack Rogers, *Jesus, The Bible, and Homosexuality: Explode the Myths, Heal the Church* (Louisville, KY: Westminster Press, 2006), 79.
86. Joe Dallas, *The Gay Gospel? How Pro-Gay Advocates Misread the Bible* (Eugene, OR: Harvest House Publishers, 2007), 206.
87. Thomas Schmidt, *Straight and Narrow: Compassion and Clarity in the Homosexual Debate* (Downers Grove, IL: InterVarsity Press, 1995), 78–79.
88. Joe Dallas, *The Gay Gospel? How Pro-Gay Advocates Misread the Bible* (Eugene, OR: Harvest House Publishers, 2007), 207.
89. John Boswell, *Christianity, Social Tolerance and Homosexuality* (Chicago: University of Chicago Press, 1980), 109.
90. Joe Dallas, *The Gay Gospel? How Pro-Gay Advocates Misread the*

Bible (Eugene, OR: Harvest House Publishers, 2007), 203–204.

91. Ibid., 204.
92. Ibid.
93. Jack Rogers, *Jesus, The Bible, and Homosexuality: Explode the Myths, Heal the Church* (Louisville, KY: Westminster Press, 2006), 89.
94. Ibid., 79.
95. Lawrence Brice, *Confident Faith in a World that Wants to Believe* (Eugene, OR: Deep River Books, 2012), 1–36.
96. Professor Mathew Lee Anderson, "Why Natural Law Arguments Make Evangelicals Uncomfortable," *Christianity Today Magazine*, April 6, 2011, 1.
97. Ibid., 2.
98. Sherif Girgis, Robert P. George, and Ryan T. Anderson, "What is Marriage?", *Harvard Journal of Law and Public Policy*, Vol. 34, No. 1, 2010. 246.
99. Ibid., 247.
100. Ibid., 249.
101. Ibid., 253.
102. Ibid., 254.
103. Ibid.
104. Ibid., 255.
105. Ibid., 259.
106. Ibid., 261.
107. Ibid., 262.
108. Ibid., 263.
109. Ibid., 265.
110. Ibid.
111. President Albert Mohler in Matthew Lee Anderson, "Why Natural Law Arguments Make Evangelicals Uncomfortable," *Christianity Today Magazine*, April 6, 2011, 2.
112. Andrew Marin, *Love Is an Orientation* (Downers Grove, IL: Inter-Varsity Press, 2009), 79–80.
113. Andrew Marin refers to a passage in Joe Dallas, *The Gay Gospel?*

How Pro-Gay Advocates Misread the Bible (Eugene, OR: Harvest House Publishers, 2007), 61–62.

114. Joe Dallas, *The Gay Gospel? How Pro-Gay Advocates Misread the Bible* (Eugene, OR: Harvest House Publishers, 2007), 30.
115. Ibid., 71.
116. Ibid.
117. Special Committee re Sexual Orientation, *Acts and Proceedings of the General Assembly* (Toronto: The Presbyterian Church in Canada, 2003), 531.
118. Ibid., 545.
119. John Howard, *John's Story* (Barrie, ON: Self-published, 2003). The author is the Rev. John Howard, an ordained minister, presently a counselor living with his family and working in Barrie, Ontario.
120. Alan Chambers, *Leaving Homosexuality: A Practical Guide for Men and Women Looking for a Way Out* (Eugene, OR: Harvest House Publishers, 2009), 19.
121. Ibid., 33.
122. Ibid., 50.
123. Ibid., 51.
124. Ibid., 52.
125. Ibid., 53.
126. Ibid.
127. Ibid., 54.
128. Ibid., 37.
129. Ibid., 60.
130. Ibid., 62.
131. Ibid., 63.
132. Ibid., 26.
133. The Church Doctrine Committee, *The Acts & Proceedings of the General Assembly* (Toronto: The Presbyterian Church in Canada, 1994), 267.
134. Harold Lindsell, *NRSV Harper Study Bible, Expanded & Undated* (Grand Rapids, MI: Zondervan, 1991), 507.
135. Kelly Patterson, "'New Era' for church where Sir John A. once wor-

shipped," *The National Post,* June 28, 2011.

136. Alister McGrath, *The Twilight of Atheism* (New York: Doubleday, 2004), 1, 2, 21–45.

137. Marney Patterson, *Suicide: The Decline and Fall of the Anglican Church in Canada* (Delhi, India: Cambridge Publishing House, 1999).

138. "The Nicene Creed (Latin: Symbolum Nicaenum) is the creed or profession of faith that is most widely used in Christian liturgy. It is called Nicene because, in its original form, it was adopted in the city of Nicaea by the first ecumenical council, which met there in the year 325." (*Wikipedia,* "Nicene Creed," http://en.wikipedia.org/wiki/Nicene_Creed.)

139. Sepros Vryonis, *Byzantium and Europe* (New York: Harcourt, Brace & World, 1967), 152.

Also Available from Dr. Lawrence Brice

ISBN: 9781937756093
Deep River Books
$13.99

Available wherever books are sold and on Kindle and Nook

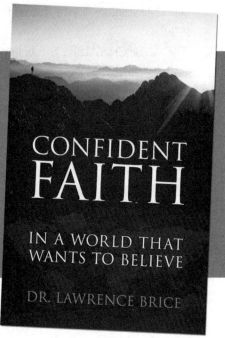

CONFIDENT
FAITH
IN A WORLD THAT WANTS TO BELIEVE

Some call God the First Cause of the universe.
Others, the Intelligent Designer... the God of the Bible...
Jesus Christ... the God Who calms life's storms.

What will you call Him?

Connect with Dr. Brice:
www.reachoutministries.net